Praise for *Sou*

Christine Wolf Hoover gently and powerfully shepherds us through a true soul journey. Reading through *Soul Adventuring* is like having a long conversation with my wise and funny friend, and I didn't want to pause at any point. Christine continues to extend hope and curiosity for what a wholehearted life can really become. I am confident that my life and family will forever reap the benefits of what I have gained through her lighthearted but clear wisdom.

> —**Stephanie Lee,** Founder and Director of You Are, Inc.
> youareconference.com

As a pastor, I spend most of my time helping people integrate God's Word into real life. I've had the privilege to learn this great work from many people I respect, but few do it with such joy, wisdom, and passion as Christine Wolf Hoover. There's rarely a week that goes by where the lessons, wisdom, and relational impact of Christine aren't felt in our family life, friendships, or church. To have so much of that wisdom packed into one great book will be a blessing to each person who joins Christine on this great soul adventure.

> —**Chris Millar,** Church Planting Pastor, The Well Community Church

I have read my fair share of self-help and inspirational books over the thirty-five years I have been a therapist. Almost all have at least a nugget of truth to be gleaned by the end. But few have such a treasure trove of wisdom and practical takeaways page after page as *Soul Adventuring*. Christine writes with a winsome and raw honesty that is congruent with who she is to her core, and she seamlessly weaves God's truth with clinical tools that are both practical and contemplative. After thirty years of friendship and a shared professional journey as therapists, I have watched Christine both "do the work" and "do the joy" that has culminated in this book that will lead readers to an authentic life of self-discovery and freedom in Christ.

> —**Susan Laukoter, MEd, LPC**, Rapha Christian Counseling

As a seasoned traveler and storyteller, Christine captivates the reader. Using personal anecdotes, she masterfully weaves lessons of faith and psychology alongside colorful, descriptive analogies. She enters complicated spaces with wisdom and clarity, effortlessly aligning evidence-based clinical tools with the truth of God's Word. The book equips readers with tools and strategies to identify and address the root causes of shame, helping them break free from its limiting effects. This is a reading adventure you won't want to miss. It may be the tool God uses to change your life!

—Ashley Hughes, Founder of Mama Needs a Manuel

While most of us want to be brave, bravery is hard. That's why this book is so needed. It's not just an invitation; it's a much-needed roadmap for living a life marked by joy rather than shame—and the courage it takes to get there.

—Josh Storie, Teaching Pastor, Fort Worth Bible Church, and author of *Common Grace*

Soul Adventuring is proof that the greatest helpers are those that generously, courageously share their personal journey towards growth, transformation, and ultimate transcendence. Neuroscience, travel adventure, therapeutic intervention, and Christian faith converge in this powerful, practical primer for uprooting shame and the harmful life patterns it evokes to embrace a joy-filled life. *Soul Adventuring* is must-read. You will refer to this book again and again for the carefully distilled wisdom that therapist and fellow sojourner, Christine Wolf Hoover, shares. Ready, set, go! Begin your soul adventure today!

—Jennifer Cumberbatch, Founder of Full Measure

Christine Wolf Hoover's title for her book describes her well—she is truly a soul adventurer. Her fresh insight into living life with God's Word as her guide is both challenging and thought provoking. We have known Christine as a wife, mother, fellow worshipper, and friend. Any time spent learning from the journey that she has traveled will be valuable for your mental, spiritual, and emotional health. This book will be a worthy addition to your library.

—Gaines West, West Webb Allbritton Gentry Law Firm, and **Susan West**

I've known Christine for many years, and her writing feels just like her personality: deep and insightful but always enveloped in joy. By addressing the root causes of shame and developing healthy coping mechanisms, *Soul Adventuring* offers practical strategies to find freedom from the ways we all get stuck trying to please, perfect, and perform. Christine weaves clinical tools and personal experiences with God's truth, leaving the reader inspired, empowered, and ready to embark on their own soul adventure.

—**Tamie Dearen,** *USA Today* bestselling author, tamiedearen.com

I have known Christine for over twenty-five years, and during that time I've seen her learn, grow, and bloom in multiple seasons of life. I traveled with her on her growth journey as a teacher, mentor, co-teacher, and then student of her amazing spiritual insights. She astonished me with her meteoric growth as a Bible teacher, due in part to her tenacious love of learning and sharing. Adding the dimensions of counseling therapy to her vast Biblical knowledge allowed her to write a book that artfully weaves the two together to provide accessible and insightful learning. Christine is fun and energetic while being thoughtful and deep: two qualities that make reading her book a delight!

—**Sharon Lee, PhD**, retired professor of Education,
Dallas Baptist University

Soul Adventuring is a deeply moving and transformative book for those who long to integrate their faith into their life. Christine Wolf Hoover's openness and vulnerability make this book stand out. She doesn't just share tools; she shares her heart. Through her own journey of challenges and triumphs, Christine invites us into a story that resonates deeply with the joys and struggles we all face. Her authenticity and courage inspire us to embrace our calling with bravery, grace, and joy. This is more than a guide; it's a companion for every person seeking to live out their faith with integrity and purpose. A must-read for those ready to embark on their own soul adventure.

—**Shaun Burrow,** PhD, A&M Christian Counseling Center Clinical Director

If you know Christine Wolf Hoover, you clearly see her indomitable spirit throughout her new book, *Soul Adventuring*. Christine swirls story after story into a clear path through the chaos of human healing and growth. She guides the reader to see further horizons while examining each step before them. Particularly timely is her understanding of shame and its debilitating effects on each of us. While our society cheers fame, self-esteem, or self-help, Christine hands out a map and compass to navigate the trail toward health. I urge you to join her on this grand adventure.

—**Richard Rogers,** DMin, Senior Pastor, University Heights Baptist Church

CHRISTINE WOLF HOOVER

MA, LPC

SOUL
ADVENTURING

Do the work - do the joy !

Christine Wolf Hoover

YOUR GUIDE TO
LIVING WITH
BRAVERY
AND JOY

Published by Courageous Heart Press
College Station, TX
CourageousHeartPress.com

Cover Design by Liz Schreiter
Editing and Interior Design by My Writers' Connection

Library of Congress Control Number: 2025930432
Paperback ISBN: 978-1-950714-49-0
Hardcover ISBN: 978-1-950714-51-3
eBook ISBN: 978-1-950714-50-6

To Madison, Landon, and Colton–

Raising the three of you has been my most beautiful adventure. Nothing makes me feel more alive than watching you live with bravery and joy.

To Chris–

The depth of your unwavering love and support surpasses every mountain we scaled, every journey we embarked upon, and every landscape we explored.

To Mom and Dad–

It was you who modeled wanderlust and showed me the magic of sleeping under the stars, awakening in me a deep love for nature and travel.

CONTENTS

Foreword 1

Author's Note 3

Part 1: The Adventure Begins

Chapter 1: An Invitation to Adventure 7

Chapter 2: The Way Forward 17

Chapter 3: Your Sacred Guide 31

Part 2: Packing Essentials

Chapter 4: Your Integrated Brain 49

Chapter 5: Your Story 73

Chapter 6: Your Emotional World 89

Chapter 7: Your Boundaries 109

Part 3: Travel Advisories

Chapter 8: The Unwanted Passenger 129

Chapter 9: Ruts That Keep You Stuck 145

Chapter 10: Roadblocks 163

Part 4: Map to New Freedom

Chapter 11: Forming Brave Soul Habits 185

Part 5: Adventure Awaits

Chapter 12: The Adventure Ahead 211

Chapter 13: Sacred Benediction 221

Appendix 227

Bibliography 231

My Sincerest Thanks 235

About the Author 239

FOREWORD

It's a joy and privilege to introduce *Soul Adventuring: Your Guide to Living with Bravery and Joy*, written by my dear friend of more than twenty years, Christine Wolf Hoover. Christine is not only a gifted therapist and teacher but also one of the most courageous and compassionate people I know. I am a more "serious" person by nature, and every time I am with Christine, her adventurous spirit awakens something inside of me. I have always said that if you look up the word *fun* in the dictionary, you will find a picture of her.

For as long as I've known her, Christine has lived with that adventurous spirit and a deep desire to walk alongside others on their journeys toward healing and wholeness. She has a gift for sharing wisdom, all while making you laugh and cry at the same time. Her willingness to explore the hard and often messy parts of life—and to invite others into that same journey—is what makes this book so special.

In *Soul Adventuring*, Christine offers a bold invitation: to embark on a soul-searching journey where we confront shame, embrace joy, and discover the bravery it takes to live fully. With her unique blend of clinical expertise, biblical wisdom, and personal vulnerability, Christine doesn't just tell us what to do; she walks the path with us. Her writing is equal parts challenging and encouraging, full of practical tools, inspiring stories, and a heartfelt commitment to helping us live freer, more joyful lives. And who doesn't want that?

In these pages, Christine lays bare her own struggles with fear and perfectionism, revealing that even those who seem brave on the outside have their own battles to fight. She courageously confronts the roadblocks that keep us stuck, especially the insidious power of shame.

But she doesn't stop there. Christine equips us with tools to move forward, tools we can use to unpack our emotional baggage, rewrite harmful narratives, and cultivate habits that lead to joy, rest, and relational wholeness.

What I love most about *Soul Adventuring* is Christine's ability to take complex truths and make them accessible and transformative. She weaves together personal stories, neuroscience, and spiritual practices to create a roadmap for growth that feels both practical and profound. Her honesty is disarming, her insights are life-changing, and her encouragement is like a breath of fresh air for the weary soul.

To read this book is to step into an adventure—one that will challenge you, stretch you, and ultimately transform you. You will laugh, you will cry, you will shout, "me too" as you follow along.

Whether you're wrestling with shame, longing for deeper joy, or simply ready to take the next step in your own soul adventure, Christine's words will meet you where you are and gently guide you forward.

I'm so grateful for Christine's voice and her friendship, and I know this book will bless and inspire you just as much as it has me. Say yes to this adventure—it's worth it.

—**Meredith Perryman**, coach, speaker, and author of *The Whole Story*
MeredithPerryman.com

AUTHOR'S NOTE

 Limitations exist in all aspects of life, including this book. My primary goal has been to present complex therapeutic and spiritual principles in a user-friendly manner. I sincerely hope I have not diluted the weightiness of either the clinical or the Christian truths about which I have written; additionally, I may have unknowingly borrowed concepts and phrases from those I have learned from over the years. I attempted to source my material well, but if I have missed citing a primary source, I extend my deepest apologies.

 For the purpose of confidentiality and client privacy, the client stories presented in this work are fictionalized names and stories, representing common therapeutic themes encountered by my clients over the years. If any names or situations in this book seem to resemble anyone you know, it is purely coincidental.

 I've created an album on my website called Soul Adventuring Scenes where you can find pictures of the scenes from each chapter. Check it out at ChristineWolfHoover.com.

 A special thanks to my husband, Chris, whose skillful illustrations grace these pages. I am grateful for the profound commitment and boundless creativity you poured into this project.

Download the Companion Guide

Get your free companion guide to *Soul Adventuring* at ChristineWolfHoover.com. The reflection questions and tools in the guide will equip you to go deeper on your soul adventure. It's perfect for personal reflection or for a small group study.

PART 1

The Adventure Begins

Get Ready for the Trip of a Lifetime

– 1 –

AN INVITATION
TO ADVENTURE

If you want to keep a secret, you must
also hide it from yourself.

——— GEORGE ORWELL ———

Before we begin our journey, I need to tell you a secret. It's a secret I tried to hide from everyone—even myself.

The secret began with my dream of inviting you on a grand adventure. A big, brave, soul adventure. I wanted to welcome you to a journey of finding courage and joy, an adventure that would be epic in every way. As your fearless tour guide, I would lead the way through scary and amazing spaces. My goal was that you and I—and anyone who joined us—would complete the adventure feeling invigorated and excited for whatever lay ahead for our incredible lives.

Adventure was calling. I knew that there was something more or bigger or braver *in* me that God wanted to bring *out* of me.

You know that feeling, right?

It's the calling or pull toward something different, new, intriguing—and maybe frightening.

Maybe . . .

> your adventure is taking your career in a different direction.
>
> you want to face an unhealed hurt.
>
> you want to quit being so hard on yourself.
>
> you want to take a risk to try something new.
>
> you are tired of feeling emotionally out of control.
>
> you want to deal with that confining feeling of insecurity, once and for all.

There are an infinite number of ways we feel drawn to add a tiny drop of goodness into the massive ocean of life. For me, the call was clear. God was leading me to write a book that would invite readers to take an adventure into their souls. I had visions of inspiring people to be brave and take new risks.

All I had to do was get down to the work of inviting.

I did the first thing "they" say to do. I said it out loud! I told my husband, our kids, plus a few good friends that I was writing a book—and why and how I hoped it would change people's lives. Sharing my grand vision seemed like the natural first step of my adventure.

Knowing what to write wouldn't be a problem; I was sure of that. For more than eleven years, I had been birthing new content in sessions with my counseling clients. Beyond that, teaching workshops and speaking at conferences supplied me with endless ideas, research, and a wealth of feedback.

All I needed to do was gather everything and write it down.

The vision felt alive, vibrant. Possible.

I began outlining. I vomited words on the page. Which is, again, what *they* say to do. "Just get it out," they said. "Get it on the page."

Soon enough, however, the excitement morphed into a dull dread. Writing sessions became sluggish. Instead of my fingers blazing the keyboard, they sat motionless and still. As I formed the themes and scenes, distraction buried them. Like a creek bed in a summer drought, the words dried up.

Feeling stuck, I asked for prayer. I went to writing retreats and took time off from work. I drove to lake houses, beaches, forests, and fields, searching for the perfect place to inspire me to capture the words swirling around my heart, mind, and soul. Oh, I even bought a special comfy writing jacket, a plush sherpa pullover that would surely make me feel like a *real* writer. I experienced grandiose moments of sacred inspiration, but the needle of progress barely budged.

The path forward eluded me. I sat frozen in front of the screen, hour after hour, month after month. No book emerged. Little paragraphs took shape here and there until the words ran dry once again. The months morphed into years. Discouragement dominated. Hope faded. I had placed numerous entrepreneurial visions on hold to bring this much-hoped-for book to completion. I was beginning to feel resentful toward the book. I poured endless hours into the deep chasm of a project that appeared to be bottomless.

I could not keep putting my life on pause. Reality replaced my dream; it was time to cut my losses and throw in the towel.

It's okay to quit things, I decided. I could run three miles multiple times a week, but running a marathon? I wasn't prepared for that. The book felt like the marathon I was incapable of running.

The Block

If a fear cannot be articulated, it can't be conquered.

— STEPHEN KING —

I opened my laptop one more time, the screen empty, my shame rising. Tears bitterly stung my eyes.

Giving up felt painful, but I would not continue to pour energy into a book I could not write. The utter nonsense of it all was deeply embarrassing.

It's one thing to be exhausted with someone in your life who is not doing what you want them to do. It's another thing to feel that way about yourself. It's a recipe for misery: a dash of frustration, a cup of contempt with a heaping teaspoon of annoyance sprinkled on top, all directed inward and bubbling over on high heat.

> # It's one thing to be exhausted with someone in your life who is not doing what you want them to do. It's another thing to feel that way about yourself.

It would be embarrassing to tell my friends and family I had given up. But I figured it would be easier to handle the humiliation of quitting than to face the misery of continuing a project I was unable to complete.

I paused to contemplate this challenging experience. What on earth had made this unbearably hard? It seemed exciting and dream-worthy, even doable at the beginning. The accumulated scraps of thoughts, scribbled notes, and unproductive years of wasted time, however, confirmed that bringing my vision to life was utterly impossible.

I suspect you have also felt overwhelmed, discouraged, and embarrassed in the face of unfulfilled dreams. What happens next can be worse: an accusatory inner voice, tossing around questions about your flaws and failings.

Why do I keep making the same mistakes, over and over?
What is wrong with me?
Why do I avoid tasks, even simple things like responding to a text?
Why can't I stop worrying?
Why is parenting so much harder than I imagined?
Why can't I get out of bed to exercise?
Why can't I forgive and move on?

Why do I commit to eating well and then find it so easy to hit the drive-through lane?

Why do I lose my temper so quickly?

I sat staring at the screen, ready to give up. I hit a wall; a Block too real to overcome. I took a few minutes to grieve the end of the project. The Block seemed malevolent and forceful, pushing me away from my goal. The Block, whoever or whatever it was, had won.

I had lost.

Feeling legitimately sad and ashamed, I gave myself the space to feel those feelings and put the long-held dream to rest. I submitted to my powerlessness in overcoming The Block. *I quit. I cannot keep doing this*, I thought.

That's when, like a bolt of lightning, a question flashed through my mind: What if I ask The Block if it has something to tell me? Is there something in The Block I need to hear? Something I need to face?

I leaned in and listened to The Block, as if it were a messenger.

At the risk of sounding too magical and *La-La-Land-ish*, I will tell you in that moment of surrender, I heard what The Block had been trying to tell me all along. Or rather, I saw it.

The Fear

We must travel in the direction of our fear.

— JOHN BERRYMAN —

With stunning clarity, I saw a vision of myself I had been unwilling to face. I saw how afraid I was. I saw myself pretending. Stuck. Hiding. Fearful.

The Block revealed a secret I hadn't realized I was keeping.

My inability to write was a symptom. Fear and shame were the cause.

How had I not known how frightened I was? The answer became clear as I remembered how I had avoided, numbed, ignored, and lied about the progress of this book—for three years. I pretended to write more than I actually wrote, wasting colossal amounts of time doing anything and everything. Except write.

My fear of failure was deeper than I dared admit. The process of writing these words has required me to take a painstaking look at things I hide, ways I pretend. All the facades and masquerades.

I wanted to show others how to live a big, vibrant life, yet I was slowly shrinking into the shadowy corners of my own shame.

I had been stuck in writing because I was stuck in life, specifically in my ability to be vulnerable about my insecurities and weaknesses. The truth is, I like being the expert who helps others untangle their lives. I hate being the one bound in knots. I was terrified of not being good enough, of producing something that would fall flat—a meager, mediocre contribution in a world full of other people's magnificent creations. My dread intensified when I imagined my words trapped in ink.

The Block was my own fear, keeping me hiding and pretending.

I thought I would help *you* overcome your obstacles and address your bad habits. I had imagined my clinical experience flowing with grace and kindness from my heart to yours to help *you* face your fear.

The vision I saw of myself during that moment of surrender, crouched in fear, brought another question to mind: *How could I inspire courage in others while I was pretending to have it all together?*

Honestly, I couldn't.

I wanted to be the expert, but up until that moment of insight, I had refused to follow my own advice. Before I could help anyone else, I had to acknowledge what was holding *me* back.

> Before I could help anyone else, I had to acknowledge what was holding me back.

The truth is, I am afraid of failing. I can be terrified of what others think of me. Sometimes I feel small in this great big world. I want to do hard things, but I don't want them to be so hard they require me to change. I don't like to reveal my vulnerability. I do not want others to see me as weak, uninformed. I dread asking for help.

The Block offered insight into my soul, but what was I supposed to do with it?

An answer came like another flash of lightning.

Tell the truth.

As it turns out, I couldn't write this book until I was wrecked by this book.

My secret is this: *I'm* the one who needed to be invited on a soul adventure. *I'm* the one who needed to be treated with grace and compassion. *I'm* the one who needed to model the honest struggle of what it takes to live a life of bravery and joy.

How could I expect you to face your fear when I had been unable to face my own? My choice was clear: either quit or face my insecurities head on. It was time to take my own advice and lean straight into what I had secretly been fearing.

As psychiatrist and author Curt Thompson wisely said, "Healing shame requires our being vulnerable with other people in embodied actions. There is no other way."

The only way for me to face my shame was to write the book, imperfections and all.

Telling the truth about my fear has been freeing. It feels good to finally admit my secret and share it with others.

Healer, heal thyself.

The Invitation

Life shrinks or expands, in proportion
to one's courage.

ANAÏS NIN

When we hide our fears, they grow more powerful. The more we languish in fear, the more territory it takes from us. Fear will create what it fears. We will spend time on this adventure looking directly into the face of our fear, staring it down. It is the only way to live a big, bold, joy-filled life. We must admit to our weaknesses, our secrets, and face the shame if we are ever going to travel beyond them.

> The more we languish in fear,
> the more territory it takes from us.
> Fear will create what it fears.

I called my stuck place The Block, but a better name would be *My Gift*. It took a long time to face it, but I am incredibly grateful I did.

My new invitation to you is this: Will you join me on *my* soul adventure? Will you allow *me* to be honest—really honest—about how hard it is to put into practice the principles that sound so easy?

Look, I know you are not here to hear me bemoan how hard it has been for me to write a book. The reason I decided to admit all of this is because I know you have secret fears too. You get stuck too. Maybe not about the same things or in the same way as I do, but I am certain there are times when you can't find your way through the big dreams you have for your life. You are not alone. *That* is why I wrote this book.

Soul Adventuring is about facing what feels hard to face, the places where we all get stuck. We will address the primacy of doing hard things, looking directly at our stories of hurt, changing old habits, and feeling uncomfortable emotions. It's also about learning how to transform shame and insecurity into something beautiful.

Although I am writing, and you are reading, we are connected through these words and stories; you have a companion along the way. This adventure is a communal one. I'll be beside you, helping you figure out what to pack and encouraging you as we navigate the obstacles that get in the way of our big soul adventures. Together, we'll find the path to joy and discover the incredible gift of living a brave, beautiful life.

Welcome to my soul adventure. To your soul adventure.

To *our* soul adventure!

You do not have to be all put together or know all the answers to make this journey. We will start right where you are. Grab your favorite cup of coffee or tea and get comfy on your couch or in your favorite reading chair. I will offer the tips and tricks and hacks and hopes I share with my clients, day in and day out. They are the same ones I use on all my adventures. I will weave clinical tools, Christ-centered truths, and practical strategies as we move forward. Talking directly to you would be way easier than typing to you (I think that is well established by now), but this is the best we've got, so it will have to do. I'm really glad you're here. It's going to be a fun ride!

– 2 –

THE WAY
FORWARD

In every success story, you will find someone
who has made a courageous decision.

—— PETER F. DRUCKER ——

ungs burning, knees aching, taking even one more step felt impossible. We leaned over to catch our breath, palms resting on our thighs. When we regained our strength, we could only manage ten steps at a time before having to stop to repeat the recovery process all over again. And again.

My husband, Chris, and I were near the top of Roy's Peak, an extremely challenging hike in Wanaka, New Zealand. We were traveling across the South Island of New Zealand in a brightly painted camper van. On this cheery morning we were facing one of the most anticipated adventures on our itinerary: a rugged 10-mile hike boasting a brutal elevation gain of more than 4,100 feet. The up-and-back trail takes most hikers between five and seven hours.

We are not hardcore hikers. We are travelers who love to hike, not hikers who love to travel. There's a big difference, especially on intense trails. Don't get me wrong, we're in good shape, but we like chips and salsa and margaritas too much for anyone to mistake us for elite athletes.

The hike had lived up to every ounce of the hype. Each bend in the path offered a gorgeous new view. For the first couple of hours, we strolled uphill through lush sheep pastures. The top of the mountain is a popular jump-off spot for paragliders, and we watched in awe as what looked like human-sized dandelion seeds drifted overhead. The day was picture-perfect. Blue skies glowed behind some of New Zealand's most stunning scenery. We timed the hike superbly, starting early in the morning while it was cool and enjoying the majority of the day without large crowds on the trail.

Three hours in, the incline drastically changed and made every step a challenge. Our bodies ached, and we slowed with fatigue. The revelry faded the same way unwrapped Christmas presents quickly lose their appeal.

Doubt crept in, and we wondered about our ability to make it to the summit.

Clouds fell on the mountain, cruelly hiding the views. The poorly marked trail offered no clue as to how much climbing remained.

Uncertain, exhausted, and feeling far less inspired than we had earlier that morning, we wondered if we should give up. Chris's knee was hurting, and I knew we were both at the brink of exhaustion. I desperately wanted us both to make it to the top. I didn't want to experience it without Chris, but he urged me on, saying he would stop and wait for me to finish without him.

Suddenly, a group of exuberant hikers rounded the corner, coming down from the peak. The cloud cover had kept them hidden until they were right in front of us. It seemed as if they had appeared out of nowhere, cheerful celestial visitors delivered from above.

They immediately recognized the look of discouragement on our exhausted faces.

With a desperate plea in my eyes, I begged for hope, yet doubt dripped from my lips, "Are we close? If we make it, will it be worth it? Are the clouds covering the view on top?"

With excitement exuding from their pores, they exclaimed, "The sky is completely clear on top. *You are so close!* Only five more minutes up and you've got it. It is so worth it; don't stop now!" Their words poured hope into our empty fuel tanks, supplying renewed energy for our steps.

Guess what we did?

We got up!

We looked toward the summit, faced the top of the peak, and took our next step.

They were absolutely correct about the clouds disappearing at the top. But they lied about it being five more minutes! It was more like forty-five. At that point, though, the we-can-do-this-energy surged through our bodies. There was no stopping us.

We reached the top, doubting we could have made it one more step, but I was breathless for a different reason.

The view. Oh, the view.

God's artistry enveloped me and filled my body and soul with wonder. How could such beauty exist? We marveled at our 360-degree sweeping view of the dramatic cliffs, blue skies, and sheep pastures below. All of it so clear, so perfect. Majestic. Sacred.

Time seemed to slow in reverence of the view.

The crisp air repaired the exhaustion in our lungs as we nestled on the edge of the peak, opened our lunch, and feasted like royalty on apples and peanut butter. It was one of the most glorious scenes I have ever witnessed.

It was also one of the most challenging experiences in all of my travel adventures.

We honestly thought we couldn't make it. The only reasons we continued to take step after excruciating step forward was the encouragement from strangers and the promise of beauty.

Welcome, my friend, to the same challenge.

The way forward is hard. You must *do your work* to live a healthy life. No one can do it for you.

In this book, instead of climbing Roy's Peak, we will scale the interior walls of our souls. Just as those climbers did for Chris and me, I will cheer you on with the truth: The journey is worth it. You *can* do it.

Beautiful, wonderful creations are hidden within you, ready to be revealed—treasures waiting to be uncovered, risks you need to take, addictions you need to release, and habits you need to break. The road we'll travel together won't always be easy. Sometimes, in fact, the way forward will feel hard, even demanding. We will labor through steps that feel uncertain, navigate challenging switchbacks, and struggle for breath when, like thin air, available resources just don't seem like enough.

> The way forward is hard. You must *do your work* to live a healthy life. No one can do it for you.

You will need to *do the work* as you traverse the deep patterns established in your soul, patterns you may yet be unaware of. Those patterns can keep you feeling small and exhausted and cause you to wander alone and confused. They can also be deceiving. Sometimes they even look like success, when in reality they are ruts of performance addiction and people pleasing.

You may feel like giving up at times, but please know this: The life available to you on the other side of this soul adventure is worth every single challenging step.

The Way Forward Is Not Hard

I get up. I walk. I fall down. Meanwhile, I keep dancing.

—————————————————— HILLEL ——————————————————

The way forward is hard. It is also true that the way forward is *not* hard.

Cynthia reached out to me for a session after a six-month hiatus. We had forged a robust therapeutic relationship over the years as we untangled her complex childhood abuse and subsequent tumultuous dating relationships. I could sense the all-too-familiar discouragement sneak into the room with her. Sadness shrouded her as she sank onto the couch.

Face tense and shoulders rigid, she finally spoke in a defeated voice. "I should be working harder. I should have read that book you told me to read," she said, self-loathing dogpiling on her despair. "I should be better by now. I know if I worked harder, I wouldn't be here. I hate that I can't change."

I looked right at her, giving her a moment to see the grace in my gaze.

"Cynthia, you *are* doing the work. But no matter how much you do, you continue to feel it is not enough work. What if we changed the way we see the work?"

In the mental health world, the word *work* is often used to describe the challenging process of emotional and relational growth. Progress requires that we "do the work."

As a follower of Jesus[1], I see this truth come to light in my faith walk as well. It requires effort to grow in faith, the same way it requires effort to develop muscles. Growing in and living out faith includes the discipline of life-giving and soul-shaping practices. It takes determination, energy, and commitment.

---

1 As a therapist, I work with clients from all faith backgrounds and with some who don't hold to faith practice. My faith permeates my life and the way I think, work, and live. That said, this soul adventure is for anyone who wants to live a bigger, bolder life. You don't have to be a Christian to apply these principles to your life.

In all aspects of both life and faith, healthy progress also demands grace.

We are works in progress, but thinking of healing and growth as *work* tends to stir up all sorts of counter-reactions. Maybe you recognize these behavior patterns in yourself:

- Doom scrolling after a hard day at work because more work sounds exhausting.
- Avoid taking positive steps toward change because it feels like the goal is impossible to ever achieve.
- Neglecting personal growth by focusing on duties that seem more time-sensitive, like doing the dishes or the yard or the laundry.

It's time we rethink what it means to *do the work*. We *work* at our jobs, *work* at our relationships, *work* at parenting. We must complete housework, yard work, paperwork, and homework.

But planning a vacation can also be a kind of work—a work we are *excited* about, knowing that sunny beaches and mountaintop experiences are ahead.

I want to invite you to see life in a new, beautiful way. As well as inviting you to *do the work*, I am also proposing you *do the joy!*

Doing the joy is about moving our lives toward goodness, toward relationships, and toward connection. Joy is the most energizing space in the brain. We feel good when we experience joy, and we always want more of it!

In his Life Model approach, which integrates neuroscience, relational principles, and theology, Dr. Jim Wilder notes, "Joy stimulates the growth of the brain systems involved in character formation, identity consolidation, and moral behavior. Based on brain characteristics, character change is best developed and maintained in joyful relationships. Joy activates the brain's social engagement system and prepares us to engage with God and others."

The social engagement system in the brain is essentially the opposite of our survival operating system (fight, flight, freeze). It equips us to be available for relational connection and emotional safety.

All through Scripture, joy is a primary theme:

- The joy of the Lord is our strength. (Nehemiah 8:10)
- Weeping may stay overnight, but there is joy in the morning. (Psalm 30:5)
- A cheerful heart is good medicine, but a crushed spirit dries up the bones. (Proverbs 17:22)
- Jesus came so that his joy would be in you and that your joy may be complete. (John 15:11)

Joy can be the work itself, just as it can be the outcome of our work. In his book *Celebration of Discipline*, theologian Richard Foster notes that "joy makes us strong."

Even with this new joy-focused perspective, doing the joy can feel like work. The one thing that will be true of all soul adventures is that the journey will be challenging and exhausting at times. It may feel uncomfortable—or miserable. When we do the joy, we won't be coasting. We will still be pushing into difficult new territory.

What I am asking is that we keep our focus on the joy, even as we look to the future. We are looking around the bend and seeing ourselves on the peak, reveling in the view. But before we get there, we are seeking and noticing beauty, progress, and growth along the way. Doing the joy is fighting your way to beauty, to delight, and to wonder. These, after all, are what our souls were made for. We need to be open to see joy. To experience it. To consume it. To bring it into our bodies.

When you finally make it to the top, doing the joy means taking time to *enjoy* the view. Allow the energy that flows from experiencing joy to lead you into emotional, relational, and spiritual wholeness.

> ## Doing the joy is fighting your way to beauty, to delight, and to wonder. These, after all, are what our souls were made for.

There's one more part to the Roy's Peak story, and it's my favorite!

After a few bites of lunch, we noticed a higher spot where a few people had carefully walked out to get pictures. It was a peak on the peak. I was intrigued! I wanted to make our way out there, to the highest of the highest spots. Content with our perch, Chris offered to stay back to get a picture of me.

After hiking the additional 100 yards across a rocky ledge to get to the precarious tip, I could barely see Chris. I knew, however, that he would be snapping pictures when I got there, so I waved across the chasm and posed for a few seconds. Then, I started jumping. Chris was not at all surprised to see me spontaneously jumping into the air; it's a family trait. Our Hoover clan has captured mid-air memories on every vacation and at every celebration. Still, we hadn't orchestrated any form of countdown for him to know when I would be up in the air, so I wasn't optimistic about the shot.

When I made my way back, Chris was grinning from ear to ear. "Look at this!" he exclaimed as he handed me his phone. I zoomed in on the picture. I was completely shocked.

He had captured it—an absolutely perfect jump. I was in mid-air, the sky behind me, wispy clouds floating above me, the peak of the peak under my bent knees. My shouts of delight floated across the valley. "I can't believe you got it! We did it!"

That is *exactly* what I want for you too.

On our soul adventure, my hope is that you will risk climbing a little farther than you believed you could, feel inspired to jump with joy, and shout to the world, "I did it!" As we embark on this journey together, each of our sceneries will be different. We all will have unique jumping off spots. Our respective routes to lives of bravery and joy will take us down different crooked roads and foggy paths.

I'll make one quick disclaimer: Joy is not the same as happiness. We can find joy all along the way, but we won't find happiness around every bend. Knowing the difference and setting the proper expectations will save you from unnecessary disappointment. Adam Grant, an organizational psychologist and Wharton professor, notes, "Being obsessed with happiness can make us unhappy. Joy doesn't arise from ruminating about emotions. It comes from immersing ourselves in worthwhile experiences. Happiness is not a goal to pursue. It's a byproduct of leading a life of meaning and engagement."

Don't just do the work. Do the joy.

Do you want to see the evidence of me *doing the joy*? Flip to the front cover. That's Roy's Peak. And me.

The Paradoxical Adventure

I've laid out a few opposing statements.

The way forward is hard. The way forward is not hard.

Do the work. Do the joy.

Are you scratching your head a little? Good. The paradox is intentional, meant to invite you to consider these truths more deeply.

The word *paradox* comes from the Greek word *paradoxos*, which combines the prefix *para* (beyond or outside of) and the verb *dokein* (to think). The idea involves combining contradictory features or qualities. George Orwell used this literary device when talking about inequality in *Animal Farm* by saying, "All animals are equal, but some animals are more equal than others." Orwell called his readers to think outside the box, to hold space for contradictory concepts at the same time.

The adventure ahead of us is paradoxical. It is a both/and kind of journey. When we live our lives fully, we will come to understand that it's only natural to experience both comfort and discomfort. This is the human condition. Beauty and brokenness. Bravery and fear. Hope and despair. Strength and weakness. Certainty and confusion. Joy and pain. Life and death.

All opposites. Yet they work together.

> When we live our lives fully, we will come to understand that it's only natural to experience both comfort and discomfort.

Paradoxes aren't only used in modern literature. Scripture is full of them. Jesus said, "the last will be first, and the first will be last"[2] and "unless a grain of wheat falls into the earth and dies, it remains alone; but if it dies, it bears much fruit."[3] One of the greatest paradoxes in the history of humanity is that for the *joy* set before him, Jesus endured the suffering of the cross.[4]

Our journey ahead is a paradox in every way. It is at the intersection of these opposing experiences where we find growth. This intersection will be a foundational element of how we will spend our time on our soul adventure. Our goal on this adventure is to live lives of bravery and delight, which means we must be willing to face the things we fear and the forces involved in robbing us of true joy.

The way forward is hard. The way forward is also not hard.

All of what I am asking you is wrapped up in these two simple phrases: Do the work. Do the joy.

Are they paradoxes? Yes.

Are they possible? Absolutely.

2   Matthew 20:16, BSB

3   John 12:24, ESV

4   Hebrews 12:2

Yay for Your Yes

The big question is whether you are going to be able
to say a hearty yes to your adventure.

— JOSEPH CAMPBELL

Our souls come alive at the irresistible invitation to fulfill the desires embedded within them. We are built, *created*, with desires for perfect intimacy, perfect relationship, like what existed in the Garden of Eden. We all have longings for connection, attention, harmony, affirmation, beauty, laughter, delight, wonder, and joy.

In *Surprised by Joy*, C.S. Lewis wrote about the German word *sehnsucht*. It has no exact English translations, but it means to have a profound longing for something unknown, like a forward-facing nostalgia. It's as if we are intensely missing something we have already experienced, yet we don't even know precisely what. It's easy to say *yes* to these soul-adventure invitations because our very beings are designed for them.

> ## Our souls come alive at the irresistible invitation to fulfill the desires embedded within them.

Even so, something else within you may be pulling you back from the edge, warning you not to dive into saying yes and embarking on this journey. The choice is up to you. Will you listen to the thoughts of fear, or will you lean into the desire to leap in with a resounding yes? Before you answer, let's do a little experiment.

Notice the difference in your body with a yes versus a no.

Scenario 1: Close your eyes. Take a few deep breaths in. Open your palms up, resting gently on your knees. Now smile and begin to nod your head up and down, pretending to be saying a cheerful "yes." In your mind's eye, envision yourself walking freely or sitting in a sunny, beautiful landscape. It could be beaches or mountains, porches or patios. Take a few moments to build the picture in your mind. Once you have it, continue with a smile, a head nod, while looking at the scene for twenty to thirty seconds. Notice what this feels like in your body.

Now, let's do it again.

Scenario 2: Close your eyes. Keep your breath shallow and tight. Close your fists, holding them at your side. Shake your head back and forth, eyebrows furrowed, pretending to be saying a determined "no." In your mind's eye, envision yourself standing or sitting at the entrance of a dark alley that has a wall at the end or an overgrown field with no path forward. Continue this for twenty to thirty seconds. Notice what this feels like in your body.

This is called embodiment work. It means paying attention to the reality of feeling life in and through our bodies. Hopefully the little experiment gave you a taste of how naturally our bodies positively respond to an invitation to beauty and delight, an invitation to a *yes*. On the contrary, how tense and tight our body becomes when responding to a *no* or an obstacle that is seen as blocking our path.

French philosopher and mathematician René Descartes said, "I think, therefore I am." The truth, however, is much deeper than what was once believed. We don't merely think our way through life. Our bodies are wise, carrying deep intuition in them. James K.A. Smith, a professor of philosophy at Calvin University, challenges Descartes's view and offers this holistic insight: "We make our way in the world by means of under-the-radar intuition and attunement, a kind of know-how that we carry in our bones. As lovers—as desiring creatures—our primary orientation to the world is visceral, not cerebral."

We are mind *and* body *and* soul. Changes of behaviors and habits can change the heart in both a physical and spiritual sense. Which means saying yes to taking the first step can be scary. But it is also thrilling.

This journey is about learning to live bigger, bolder, and more joyfully, and it is not one you must travel alone. As we begin this journey together, I encourage you to invite Jesus to join you on this adventure. As you say yes to moving past the fear and hurt and other obstacles that have kept you stuck, he is eager to join you on the journey to fulfilling the desires God planted within the whole of you. All you have to do is ask.

God can heal our hurts, redeem our sin patterns, and speak truth to the stories we tell ourselves about ourselves. Immediately after a person with leprosy cried out to Jesus for healing, Jesus responded with a resounding yes. "Jesus reached out and touched him. 'I am willing,' he said. 'Be healed!' And instantly the leprosy disappeared" (Mark 1:41, NIV).

Jesus will always say *yes* to you when you say *yes* to becoming more of who you were created to be.

So, yay for your *yes*! I'm excited to be on this soul adventure with you!

Do the Work

Tell someone the dream/project/healing you want to face. What is one small step you need to take to begin this adventure? Write it down and do it.

Do the Joy

Name one quality of your personality you are proud of. Write it down by saying, "One of the things I value most about myself is _____."
Reflect on the quality and enjoy the positive feelings.

YOUR SACRED GUIDE

When setting out on a journey, do not seek advice
from someone who never left home.

— RUMI —

Amanda sat on my counseling couch, sobbing uncontrollably. She was in her early thirties, and her small frame heaved in grief as her entire body experienced the sorrow from the years of trauma, childhood neglect, and broken relationships.

"I've never mattered," she whispered as she wept. "To anyone."

"I'm here," I quietly responded. Staying with her in her grief, I assured her I was available. I couldn't say I knew exactly how she felt. I didn't have her memories, her story, but I could be a witness to the pain she was experiencing. "Ride the wave. Let yourself feel it," I told her. "You've got this. I'm with you."

Her sobbing continued, a cathartic release of decades of repressed sadness. She looked up to see the tears in my eyes. She saw me as I saw her. It was a sacred moment.

Two years later, Amanda and I sat together, fondly remembering that moment. Now she sits more upright on the couch, the bond between us strong and sturdy. When she first showed up in my office, wrecked by pain and loss, her eyes rarely met my gaze. Her circumstances haven't changed much, but she has learned how to welcome her grief, her loss, her pain. She is writing a new story for her life. It continues to be peppered with sorrow, but she faces her life with grit. With bravery. With joy.

I consider it to be one of the greatest privileges to be a sacred listener to fellow travelers like Amanda. I pray every morning as I walk to my car, *Lord, let me honor the sacred stories of the people in my presence today.* Stories of betrayal, hopelessness. The places where relational storms have ravaged, where the road is covered in debris, making it difficult to see the path forward.

Not everyone who sits on my couch is in crisis. Some come for what I call soul maintenance, checking to make sure their inner engine is running smoothly. I consider their journey equally sacred. It is my great honor to hold space for people's stories. I've listened to literally thousands of stories of heartbreak, shame, confusion, rejection, and insecurity.

I can't be your sacred listener, but I will be your sacred guide. Now, *sacred* can sound serious, stuffy, and stained-glassy, but I hope you know by now that serious and stuffy are not my vibe. Nor do I have secret access to God.

When I offer to be your sacred guide, I use the word to express the sense of reverence, honor, and connection I feel for you. My hope is that in these pages, you will find the same honoring of your story, of your life, of your joys and pains.

I am a sacred guide because your story is sacred.

Your life is sacred.

You are sacred.

Our soul adventure is a pathway to dream big, form deeper relationships, experience less anxiety, and build a life filled with laughter and joy. Soul work is like any adventurous hike. The most spectacular views come from taking one little step at a time, one annoying switchback at a time, one water break at a time. And it helps to have a good companion at your side to cheer you on as you traverse that rocky trail or leap off a cliff into sparkling soul-refreshing pools below.

In all the personality tests, I'm the one looking for fun, travel, people, dreams, parties, unicorns, and fairy dust. I love to say yes to a dare and take the road less traveled. As your guide, I'll ask you to take risks. To lay it out there. To travel to some stunning places where you can take in the wonder of who God built you to be, to peer into the most uncharted cavern in all the world: your soul. And here's what I know about you: You are not here by accident. You are here because you are longing for something.

We all are.

We long to be heard and seen. We long to be free from hurts and pain, to be our true self. And we are all afraid, at times, of the road ahead.

One of my most crucial jobs as a therapist is similar to that of a trail guide. My role is to stay focused and clear on where we are headed. I point the way for my clients' souls to be brave and to be set free. I clip on the safety harnesses so the client is safe to leap off the cliff of their fears into the open air to find what their soul desires. My job is to hold the space for them to face what they fear the most. Because, truth be told, we all want to be challenged to take risks. Despite the fear, we know, deep down, that we are made for adventure, risk, wonder, and beauty.

The Roads That Shape Us

As your sacred guide, I will direct us toward a life of bravery and joy. Beyond that, my hope is to guide you through your soul adventure, back to where it belongs: at home with a good God who will tend to your soul far better than I ever could.

Many years of private practice as a trauma-informed psychotherapist, twenty-plus years of Bible teaching, and years of hard-knock insights from raising three great kids have helped prepare me for this journey. Add to that the experience that comes with being a Honey (my grandma name) and from decades of travel adventures, forty-plus years of friendships, and thirty-plus years of marriage, and I can certainly say my soul adventures to date have been beautiful. I also have a few bruises and scars from the bumps and mishaps along the way.

Chris and I have been married since 1991. We met in 1990 when he was a newbie hire at a restaurant where I was a trainer. He was determinedly cutting up tomatoes when I burst in through the back door to tell all my restaurant friends about my blue Buick Cutlass Supreme being stolen for the third time. (It was stolen two more times after that. You need to hear that story but not right now. It's a good one that includes cassette tapes, roller skates, and a grass skirt.)

Chris is truly the best of the best. He is the most faithful partner I could ever ask for, and I live in awe of his goodness toward me. His heart is pure and tender. His eyes are a magical blue, bright with delight, and he desperately wants to alleviate suffering in the world. He has been in full-time ministry all these years. Our deepest joys and no doubt some painful heartbreaks have come from church ministry.

Our sweet little family has been the greatest adventure of my life. Our kids, Madison, Landon, and Colton, burst into our world with beautiful chaos, all three born in less than three short years. I look at our adult kids with awe and wonder. They picked perfect partners for their lives, enriching our family even more. How did we do it? How did such amazing humans make their way in this world through us? It was, of course, our imperfect faith in a wholly perfect and loving God, supplemented by family and friends beside us every step of the way. And loads of laughter.

Speaking of faith, I'm convinced we have the best companion in Jesus, whom Scripture calls Immanuel, *God with us.* This incarnational God, the one who came in the person of Jesus, promises to never leave us.

It's okay if you are not all that certain about Jesus. I sit with people all day from every faith walk imaginable; there are no expectations of where you need to be spiritually. My longing is that you feel welcomed into this sacred space, a place where we can both practice new ways to be brave and forge new pathways for joy.

And yes, I still need the practice. Even with my experience, I'm a guide with some messes of my own.

Let me explain.

Your Work-in-Progress Guide

We need to be guided by people who are walking the direction we need to go, ever so imperfectly. The offer to be your guide is not one birthed out of arrogance, but out of honesty. Theologian Henri Nouwen said true spiritual leaders are "willing to put their own faith and doubt, their own hope and despair, their own light and darkness at the disposal of others who want to find a way through their confusion and touch the solid core of life." We need people who are willing to take a risk to walk ahead of us, name their own sins, face their own destructive patterns, and show us the way forward.

Speaking of naming destructive patterns, I tell this story with a heap of hesitation. It reveals the darker sides of my soul I would rather keep tucked away from view. But if I can invite you to jump off a cliff, I must be brave enough to show up here as my authentic, work-in-progress self.

This happened a couple of years ago. It started with a good cup of coffee and a mindless morning scroll on social media.

As I was scrolling, I saw quotes posted from a book I hadn't heard of before. The quotes were similar to how I spoke to my clients and ways in which I encouraged them. I did a quick Google search, read the summary, and discovered the basic content of the book matched many of my recent trainings. When I saw the book title, I was annoyed, jealous, and frustrated. I was already in the process of outlining this book, and the waves of writing paralysis had begun to smash the shores of my creativity with stunning force.

Oh, the irony of ironies. I was paralyzed in writing a book that evidently had already been written.

Here existed a book successfully articulating much of the content I was envisioning. It was finished, highly regarded, and already making an impact on many people. Adding injury to insult, the author seemed way smarter than me. Of course.

The other book: published.

My book: literally a mess, scattered in a thousand different places, half-baked, and half-written. To add even more salt to my slimy wound, the author was years younger with similar credentials.

My thoughts swirled with self-condemnation. He wrote my book! And of course, people love it. Proof I can't do it, and it's too late for me to even try. This is what I get for being lazy and lame. I'm little, the world is big, and I won't ever show up to make my mark.

The feelings that arose in me poked at the nagging fear that maybe what was meant for me had passed me by. Worse yet, it seemed to pass me by because of my own deep flaws. It felt as if I was not committed enough to do what I was supposed to do and not good enough for the task in front of me.

Here's the kicker: Celebrating other's successes is a strong value of mine. I long to see my fellow humans show up to their lives with their gifts and talents. It is one of the primary reasons I was in the process of writing, although stuck in procrastinating, this book.

At that moment, though, I was not the kind of person I wanted to be. It felt like the author had beaten me in a race I had barely started. I was the runner stumbling at the starting block, ashamedly walking off the track alone while the crowd cheered for the winner.

Sometimes my heart can be small and bound up tight like the Grinch's. I can be envious and insecure. The author's success felt like a neon arrow pointing at me, buzzing and blinking, *Christine, look at what you didn't do. Christine, look at what you didn't do.*

It's hard to admit when our inner world doesn't match up with our values, isn't it? It can be painful to confess the waywardness of our hearts.

Your insecurities may lie elsewhere, but I bet you understand the uncomfortable reality of seeing unkindness, jealousy, comparison, judgment, or pettiness show up in you. Maybe you see someone who you think looks healthier than you, and you shame yourself for what you ate for dinner. Maybe you see how your coworker handles a work situation, but you secretly roll your eyes because you think you could do it better.

The truth is, we are all works in progress. There is no other way to be human. This wisdom from Henri Nouwen pushes me to shine the light on my flaws: "The main question is not 'How can we hide our wounds?' so we don't have to be embarrassed, but 'How can we put our woundedness in the service of others?'"

Here we find more paradoxes slapping us in the face:

Sacred and incomplete. Healed and still being healed. Mature and yet immature. Wounded yet useful.

We are all a mixture of courage and fear, security and insecurity, humility and pride.

I'll tell you what, though, we cannot let our stories end when our mess shows up, when it becomes evident we are a work in progress. My story *did not* end with my jealousy and insecurity. I did something crucial in that moment. I faced the messy stuff in my soul, using both bravery and joy to help dredge my way to a healthier place. I handled my wayward emotions a little like country life taught me to deal with bees.

Speaking of country life, I doubt you have ever heard of Arneckeville, Texas. It's the humble, rural, close-knit community in south central Texas where I learned to be me. There is no census count anymore, but it's still on the map. You can find it south of Austin, north of Corpus Christi.

Arneckeville has more cows than people and more fence posts than cows. It's where I learned to skip rocks, speak respectfully to adults, and help a distressed cow stuck in labor. To help birth that baby calf, my dad would stick his arm where I thought no human should stick their arm. Then he hooked a chain around the calf's ankle, and we pulled with all our might. I won't even begin to describe the horror of butchering chickens. The term *running around like a chicken with its head cut off* has a very literal meaning to me and still brings to mind images that are half comical and half terrifying.

I grew up a tomboy in the truest sense, my older brother Michael being my best playmate and friend. To this day, I am still so proud to be his little sister. We lived the quintessential childhood of country kids in the seventies and eighties. We floated down the Guadalupe River in aired up tractor tire tubes, raised chickens, pigs, and steers in 4-H and FFA, helped our dad haul hay, played Pong on the Atari, and kept each other's secrets pretty darn well.

I met Jesus in our little white picturesque church that you had to cross three cattle guards to get to. My great-great-great-grandfather planted Zion Lutheran Church of Arneckeville when he came from Germany in 1850, allegedly making him the first Lutheran pastor in Texas. He is buried thirty yards from my grandpa, in the quaint cemetery behind the church. Our kids were the fourth generation to be baptized in that charming little place. The community continues to function in the simpler, slower way of doing things: Friends stop by the house unannounced to find an unlocked screen door and sweet tea, a neighbor calls to tell my dad when his bull is out, and dominos are played with the seriousness and precision of an Olympic sport.

It's as peaceful as it is idyllic, with cattle grazing in the pastures and giant oak trees silhouetting the landscape at sunset. Country life taught me about how all of nature works together. Sparrows and robins eat insects that could eat holes in the tomato plants. Ladybugs take care of aphids. Beetles and earthworms break down organic matter into soil. Cow poop makes awesome fertilizer. Bees are essential pollinators, enabling plants to reproduce.

Back to my emotional storm of my book I thought someone else wrote. Back to how I have learned to handle emotions a little like bees.

Emotions, like bees, can serve us well if we slow down to listen to them. Bees are not to be feared. I learned not to freak out and start swinging at them. No need to scream and run around like a wild child. That will do you no good. The more of a fuss you make, the more likely one of them is going to zoom with a vengeance, aiming that stinger right at you.

Instead of yelling or running from those venomous emotions, I noticed and named them. I noticed the smallness of my heart, the jealousy, insecurity, fear. The emotions were strong, but rather than yield to them, I chose to do the right thing in the midst of them. Leaning into the discomfort in my soul, I offered a prayer of blessing to the author, thanking God he wrote such a helpful book. I refused to let the emotions define me. Those feelings of jealousy did not make me a jealous person.

The emotions had a message for me. The message was *not* that someone else wrote my book. The message was *not* that I am a jealous, insecure person. The message was this: The feelings arose in me because I had a book in me.

They were an indicator on the dashboard of my life saying, "There is more in you. Don't stop." The feelings were pointing to a deeper purpose in my life. No one else *would* write my book. No one *could* write my book.

The same is true for you. As your work-in-progress guide, I will point you in the direction of finding what your soul is made for. I love the way Elizabeth Gilbert, in her book *Big Magic*, invites us to dig deeper into our purpose: "The universe buries strange jewels deep within us all, and then stands back to see if we can find them. The hunt to uncover those jewels—that's creative living. The courage to go on that hunt in the first place—that's what separates a mundane existence from a more enchanted one."

Your Wounded-in-Battle Guide

My commitment for our journey is to help you navigate the rough spots of your life because I've faced potholes on my own bumpy path. We will get wounded in life in different ways, the skirmishes leaving their scars. Who better to help us heal those wounds than ones who know their way around the battlefield?

I'm here with you, fellow traveler, as your wounded-in-battle guide.

Like I said earlier, Chris and I have been in church ministry our entire marriage. That's thirty-plus years. For the most part, we've had beautiful experiences. Deep relationships and shared visions. Nevertheless, it only took one painful experience to leave us cynical and disenfranchised, almost hurt enough to walk away from it all. Our story is as complicated as a knotted pile of yarn, impossible to know where one thread starts and another stops. Untangling it here is impossible. And unnecessary.

A brief bird's-eye view will have to do.

After ten years of ministry as the worship arts pastor of our church, Chris was asked to resign his position. It was sudden and shocking, the result of a complicated leadership clash, with rival factions and painful rumors deepening the pain. Like a dirty bomb, the messy and painful explosion in our lives scattered shrapnel that left emotional scars on our souls. I stumbled through the smoky battlefield, looking for fragments of our life I could retrieve, trying to piece it back together.

No one wins those types of wars.

It wasn't just Chris' job. It was our church. It was *my* life. It was our *kids'* lives too. The church youth group was their place of connection. And it was all gone. I staggered off the battlefield of a war that wasn't mine, streaked with dirt and sweat, wounded and weary.

My view of God as a safe and reliable God was deeply affected. I wasn't sure if I could trust him. I had prayed over the situation at our church, and yet it seemed the worst-case scenario had played out.

You know that feeling, right? It may not be the same kind of church hurt, but a feeling that the entire path—ahead and behind—is riddled with danger. Looking around at a life you don't even recognize and wondering where God is in all of it.

Experiences that leave spiritual wounds can damage our view of God. They can hamper our ability to live with bravery and joy. Self-protection and self-reliance become an unhealthy focus that keep us from seeing beyond our current circumstances.

Maybe your family's strict legalism strangled the joy out of life, or you saw a church make some hurtful decisions. It could be God didn't seem to show up for you like you begged him to. Maybe you were wounded by someone who claimed to be a follower of God. Maybe a significant grief left you wondering if God is even trustworthy. I want to say this with as much compassion as I can transmit through these flat, typed words: If you have experienced anything like that, I am so sorry. I truly am. When our wounds are spiritual, it creates a deep, deep pain, cutting to the core of the trust needed to build a strong spiritual foundation. Hurt like that can affect the way you view God.

I get it. I have experienced some of those wounds. I have also been healed from some of those wounds as well. When it was all happening, my doubts were much like those that Susan and Lucy voiced about Aslan in *The Lion, the Witch and the Wardrobe,* before the Pevensie children met him.

> **Susan**: "Is he—quite safe? I shall feel rather nervous about meeting a lion."
>
> **Mrs. Beaver**: "If there's anyone who can appear before Aslan without their knees knocking, they're either braver than most or else just silly."
>
> **Lucy**: "Then he isn't safe?"
>
> **Mr. Beaver**: "Safe? . . . Who said anything about safe? Course he isn't safe. But he's good. He's the King I tell you."

Today, more than a decade after Chris lost his job, I can see God's goodness toward us throughout the entire process. I can see a sturdiness in myself as well. The pain affected how I saw God. My view of God changed, but God never did. He showed me grace and patience as we rebuilt our lives, and he will do the same for you.

Even as an experienced guide, I can't hurry you along in that healing process. More than that, I have no desire to do so because I know the work God is doing in you and for you is necessary—and it takes time.

In the chapters ahead, we will dig to uncover the adventures God has placed in you, challenges he is inviting you to face, pain he is able to heal, and emotional messes he can untangle. It will take as long as it takes, and that is just as it should be.

So that's me. A sacred guide, a work-in-progress guide, a wounded-in-battle guide. Someone who is, despite our unique stories, probably a lot like you. As sacred and scarred sojourners, we will move forward together.

I must warn you: Sometimes our progress will feel slow. Snail's pace slow. But slow change is better than no change. Starting is better than not starting. Moving one step is better than not moving at all.

Our job is to get moving—in the right direction. A recent exchange with a client who felt discouraged by the slow pace of his change proves that last point.

> **Me:** Let's say I want to go to Dallas. I get in my car and drive 90 mph south. Will I end up in Dallas? (For context, I live in Huntsville, Texas, which is directly off Interstate 45, the north-south thoroughfare in our part of the state. Dallas is to the north, and Galveston is to the south.)
>
> **Client:** No.
>
> **Me:** But I am driving fast, right?
>
> **Client:** Yes.
>
> **Me:** Driving fast and heading south means I will never make it to Dallas. I will end up in Galveston.
>
> **Client:** Or the Gulf of Mexico.
>
> **Me:** True. Let's say we live in a world where there are safe sidewalks near all the freeways. What happens if I walk north on the sidewalk? Will I make it to Dallas?
>
> **Client:** Sounds miserable.
>
> **Me:** I know it does. However, I didn't ask about my comfort. The question is, would I make it to Dallas?
>
> **Client:** I suppose so.

Me: Correct. If I go slowly and walk north, I will most definitely make it to Dallas. It would be hard, but I will arrive where I intended to arrive.

Direction is what matters, not speed. But . . .

Imagine we *were* walking—or hiking—the long road set before us. Would it change the way you pack for the trip? Of course, it would. No matter how physically fit you are, you can only carry so much for so long before the load becomes too heavy. But you can't set out without at least some essential provisions.

Packing for the Journey

The gear any adventurer carries—or forgets to pack—can make or break the trip. Sure, there are some things you can pick up along the way or get by without, depending on where you're headed and for how long. Soul adventuring, however, is not about *getting by*. It's about becoming more of who you are. It's about finding and experiencing more joy and delight every day. Since nothing feels less joyful than wearing your wet socks on a ten-mile hike because they're the only pair you've got or heading to an international destination without your passport, we need to talk about what to pack for this adventure.

Let's Go!

When it comes to packing, I cram more than I fold. I'm sure you are not surprised by that.

Two pairs of shorts, two pairs of shoes, one pair of jeans, one skirt, five shirts, and a few other necessities. Plus one big book. Crammed in a backpack. That's it.

That was all I packed for more than three months of traveling in Europe.

I had to choose wisely what made it into my backpack. No room for extra items since I would be lugging it on my back all summer. I needed to take the essentials, and whatever I packed had to be versatile enough to work in diverse circumstances.

It was 1989. I was finishing my undergraduate degree at Texas A&M University, with only a few hours left to complete my degree. Eight hours of Spanish, to be exact. I had a couple of options: I could take all eight hours in summer school classes on campus, or I could join the Spain study abroad group. Nothing sounded more awful than finishing those hours in back-to-back summer sessions in boring lecture halls. On the other side of the coin, nothing sounded more tantalizing than traveling to Spain for those final credits.

Spain it was!

When it comes to travel, I'm a whole lot like the mouse in the children's book, *If You Give a Mouse a Cookie.* The opening line reads, "If you give a mouse a cookie, he'll want some milk to go with it." Well, if you buy Christine a ticket to Spain, she'll want an unlimited European train pass to go with it. If you buy her a train pass, she'll want to hop on some boats to Greece. If she hops on some boats to Greece, she'll want to sleep on a roof in Corfu. If she sleeps on a roof in Corfu, she'll want to camp in a hut in Santorini. If she stays in Greece a little longer, she will want to avoid the treacherous after-college job hunt by staying a few more weeks.

Europe it was, June to September!

I'm not the best packer, truth be told. It's the part of travel I dread most. Typically, I start by throwing everything I think I *might* need into a suitcase, piling it high. When it is time to leave for the trip, I go back through all the items in the suitcase, taking out what I don't need. As it turns out, the same is true when it comes to writing about what to pack. After piling this section with loads of content, I had to go back to determine exactly what we truly need. I pared it down to just four pieces of essential gear.

Let's circle back to those few items I chose to put in my backpack for that summer trip to Europe. I mentioned a big book. Let me tell you a little about that book.

My backpacking trip happened long before the days of cell phones, GPS, travel blogs, YouTube, and social media. You know, back in the dark ages when we used paper maps and had to use phone booths and prepaid cards to call home. For my travel guide, I packed the book every college backpacker purchased in the 1980s: *Let's Go: Europe*. It was the bible for the budget traveler, loaded with country-by-country details, insider tips, maps, popular backpacking hangouts, all the must-dos for the major cities, and cheap hostel lodging options. (My budget was $20 a day, including lodging!) It had details to help get around cities, towns, and the countryside. It even had a section to help you say, "*I'm lost!*" in fifteen different languages. How handy is that?

The book weighed almost as much as everything else I packed.

Packing for big trips requires foresight and discernment. The same holds true for our soul adventure. In fact, the packing you'll be doing is really the first step of the journey. It's that important. Our adventure is well on its way. Growth and healing are available each step of the way, each turn of the page.

The next section will guide you like *Let's Go: Europe* guided me. I would not have found my way around all those countries without it. The next four chapters will ensure you are mentally and emotionally prepared to navigate your way through healthy, vibrant soul care. The essential gear you'll be packing are things you can use every day as you move toward the wholehearted, joy-filled life you're seeking.

Let's get to packing!

Do the Work

Name an area where you have felt "wounded in battle." God promises in Isaiah 61 to bring healing. Read Isaiah 61:1–3. Write a prayer, asking God to remind you of his promise to you.

Do the Joy

Every day this week, write a list of five things in your life that bring you joy. Share the list with a friend.

PART 2

Packing
Essentials

What to Bring on
Your Soul Adventure

– 4 –
YOUR INTEGRATED BRAIN

If there is no struggle, there is no progress.

——— FREDERICK DOUGLASS ———

I didn't know I could jump that high.

I was on a run in my beautiful east Texas neighborhood, air pods in, listening to my favorite running playlist. All was well in the world. Suddenly, without any forethought, my body leaped into the air with a finesse and brilliance I didn't even know was possible. I jumped at least three feet up and landed four feet in front of where my next step would have been. I paused my music, turning around to look back at where my running shoes had left the pavement, perplexed and puzzled. What on earth had just happened?

Why had I jumped so high and so far, without even knowing I needed to jump?

As I gathered my faculties, I glanced down. Then I saw it.

A snake. Coiled up, venomous, ready to strike.

A copperhead, to be exact. Lying exactly in the place where my foot *would have* landed if I had continued at my normal pace. The unexpected ballet leap had kept me from landing directly on the creature. The miraculous nature of the entire four-second event left me standing there in awe, eyebrows lifted, chin dropped, mouth wide open.

How had I jumped over something I had no recollection of seeing? I had saved myself from something my conscious self didn't even know I needed to avoid. My brain told my body to jump before I had any actual awareness I needed to jump. My brain responded without my permission.

Thank God.

How is this possible?

The answer lies in the unique and diverse functions of the small, yet powerful organ protected by those thick skulls of ours.

Your brain, more specifically your *integrated brain,* is the first essential you'll need for your soul adventure. I will talk more about what those two words mean together, but first, let's look at four traits that make your brain amazing.

1. Your brain can change.

Before 1990, researchers had two approaches to understanding how the human brain functioned. One was to open the skull and poke on the brain while the patient was awake. The invasive prodding, obviously, came with risks. I don't know about you, but I don't really want someone opening up my brain to see how it works. The other option was to study a dead brain. Scientists attempted to understand a firing and wiring system that was no longer firing and wiring. Sounds a bit unproductive, doesn't it?

Then a new technology called FMRI (functional magnetic resonance imaging) changed everything in the early 1990s. With FMRI, researchers could watch brain activity in a non-invasive way. The brain became the newest frontier since space exploration. Formerly unknown regions of the brain could be seen functioning in real time. The findings in the field of neuroscience have changed what we know about how humans relate, some of which includes how emotion moves through the entirety of the brain's wiring system, how the body stores trauma, and how the stress-threat response system operates below the conscious awareness.

The field of interpersonal neurobiology, which explores how a person's brain, mind, and relationships interact to shape who the person is, brought even more clarity. The title interpersonal neurobiology (IPNB) was coined by Dr. Dan Siegel, whom we can thank for his groundbreaking work to combine the fields of neuroscience, psychology, anthropology, and biology, among others.

The pioneering work coming from the field of IPNB continues to teach us the brain science behind how and why we respond in normal, everyday situations. It has opened the door to understanding the instinctual drive for human connection, the need for healthy relationships, the bonds we create through our attachment system, and the powerful impact of mindfulness. This field of study provides crucial information in understanding how to navigate our lives as caring, loving, joyful, wholehearted human beings. Most importantly, these insights reveal that it's possible to learn new ways to respond when we understand the basics of how our brain interacts and operates beyond the conscious level.

I won't bore you with an enormous amount of technical information, but the bottom line is that the brain is made to adapt. Your brain is a complex, multifaceted organ that was designed to change, create, form habits, build and sustain relationships, and keep you safe. These amazing capabilities can explain why I jumped from that snake while running, and even more interesting, why I jump when I see a stick that remotely resembles a snake.

While we're on the subject of reptiles, let's talk about lizard tails.

Do you remember being told as a kid that a lizard could grow its tail back? I'm not proud to admit I probably pulled off more than my fair share of lizard tails, being the curious little country girl I was.

As humans, we are not able to grow back tails, but our brains are built to recreate.

Neuroscience's most fascinating discoveries include the brain's remarkable neuroplasticity—its capacity for network growth and reorganization. Long before the era of neuroscience, Socrates said, "The secret of change is to focus all of your energy not on fighting the old, but on building the new." With the more recent technological advancements in brain science, we can see the truth of this statement in real time. I was introduced to the vast processes involved in brain functioning in my training to become a trauma-informed therapist through the Eye Movement Desensitization and Reprocessing therapy protocol (EMDR). EMDR allows clients to process traumatic events and distressing experiences. Brain scans taken after EMDR reveal growth in the brain's limbic area, where implicit memories are sequenced and integrated. The brain can change!

The brain's complex wiring and firing system is built to create new neural networks, which gives the brain the ability to adapt and evolve over the course of a lifetime. *Complex* is an understatement. The number of neurons firing in the nervous system alone is staggering. David Eagleman, in his book *Incognito*, explains that "A typical neuron makes about ten thousand connections to neighboring neurons. Given the billions of neurons, this means there are as many connections in a single cubic centimeter of brain tissue as there are stars in the Milky Way galaxy."

All of that complexity is sitting directly north of our shoulders, and we rarely give it the awe and wonder it deserves.

Your brain is *always* gathering new information and making adjustments—changing. Which means *you* can change.

> Your brain is *always* gathering new information and making adjustments—changing. Which means *you* can change.

I've seen proof of this in my own life. The very fact that I did not give up on this book is evidence that change in the brain is possible. My tendency, throughout my life, has been to start projects at a faster rate than I finish them. Follow-through has always been a challenge for me. My years of unfinished projects are a cluttered pile of potential.

In 2017, after our daughter Madison's wedding, I felt the need for a new project. My time and mind had been consumed with trips to and from the Dallas-Fort Worth area to help Madison decide on flowers, dresses, table linens, and seating arrangements. I was looking for something to fill those hours and wanted to do something *different*, learn something *rugged*.

It suddenly seemed exceedingly significant that I had no idea how to build a box. Surely woodworking was a competency I needed to learn. I had a strong urge to tie my hair up in a red polka dot bandana, find a denim shirt, flex my biceps, and channel Rosie the Riveter with some Christine-Can-Do-It energy.

Yes, I know my choice of project sounds impulsive and random. Truth be told, the wiring in my brain does indeed fire a wee bit on the spontaneous side.

As it just so happens, my husband, Chris, is an incredible wood-worker. A patient one, I might add. I spouted out to him my barely hatched vision of becoming a carpenter, hammer already in hand. He knows me well, so he was a tad suspicious of said vision. He is King of the Land of Optimists, however, and he took me at my word. He would help however I needed.

Game on.

I reached for some nails, ready to start, but Chris stopped me and asked me to sketch a plan of what I wanted to make. That sounded incredibly boring. I wanted to build, not draw! Eager to be a good little student for my patient instructor, I obliged. I grabbed a pencil and drew the lines and dimensions as best as I could. Next, I rummaged through the scrap wood pile to find what I needed. I measured the pieces and cut each one according to the measurements written on the dumb sketch he made me draw. I hammered a couple of nails, making one of the sides. Look at me go.

The next morning I strolled into the garage, coffee in hand, to survey the progress. The pieces I had nailed together looked sloppier than I remembered, like they didn't fit exactly right. Suddenly the project seemed messy and hard. My Rosie the Riveter energy rapidly subsided, then evaporated altogether.

If you need a hint as to what happened next, I'll leave it at this: I still don't know how to build a box. There is a partially nailed side of a box somewhere in Chris's wood pile. My quickly hatched plan was dead on arrival.

I have long wondered if I would *ever* be able to push myself to complete a long, hard project. My deeply rooted pattern of avoidance has sabotaged many of my dreams and goals. You may think I didn't build the box because I can be impatient, impulsive, distracted, unmotivated. All of those things are true, but those realities don't simply exist in my personality; they exist in the way my neurons wire and fire.

The point of knowing your brain is built to change is understanding that you *can* lean in and do new things. Things that are hard. You can change. You are built with the potential to create new habits and new ways of moving in the world.

There is no box, yet here you are, reading this book—the outcome of doing something long. Something hard.

Let's take a moment to shift from science to our souls. One of the greatest obstacles my clients face is the fear that they can't change. I am intimately familiar with this fear myself.

We make the same kinds of mistakes, face the same types of struggles, over and over. Do you ever get stuck in cycles like these?

- You are tired of trying to make everyone happy all the time.
- You feel persistent guilt about what you did or didn't do.
- You are resentful of always helping other people but never having your own needs met.

- You made a mistake years ago but now feel you are unworthy of good things.
- You feel numb and disconnected, floating above your life as it drifts past you.

It's frustrating, isn't it? To know you're repeating undesired behaviors and recycling hurtful thoughts and emotions. I'm here to say that your brain is built to change. Which means we can hold on to the hope that those cycles and behaviors don't have to continue.

Your brain can—and does—change, moment by moment, thought by thought. Neurons fire in new ways as you take in information and experience life; in fact, your brain's wiring is different now from what it was before you picked up this book. The new connections make you a slightly different person from who you were even moments earlier.

The fact that the brain *can* change doesn't make transformation easy, only possible. Even so, we have hope that the adventure of living a brave life is within reach because we are not built to stay stuck. We are built for re-creation.

Long before brain scans, the prophet Isaiah said, "Yet you, Lord, are our Father. We are the clay, you are the potter; we are all the work of your hand" (Isaiah 64:8, NIV).

Clay is moldable. It can be shaped, formed, and rebuilt.

God designed your brain for change, for renewal. For redemption.

Don't give up on that area of *stuckness*. Things can be different. You can be different.

> God designed your brain
> for change, for renewal.
> For redemption.

2. Your brain loves habits.

Your brain was wired for change, but it is also designed to conserve energy. It does not want to use extra energy to find a new way through every single situation. It is built to form efficient and easy-to-access habits, creating patterned ways of thinking, feeling, and behaving.

These patterns give the brain a reliable pathway to respond in a similar way to similar situations without having to expend new energy in that moment. Habits are automated. Let me tell you something about that brain of yours: it *loves* habits! Patterns are quick, and for this reason, the brain seeks to automate as much as possible.

The brain is a habit-forming organ. What fires together, wires together.

Julia came to see me at the cusp of turning forty. She was happily married to a man she loved, but she knew something deep inside her was unavailable to her family. She was reactive and easily angered. Regret and remorse followed each outburst in a spiral of self-condemnation. Confused by the swirling chaos of her emotions, she sought counseling because she wanted to understand herself better and relate in a healthier way to her husband and daughters.

As we explored her story, Julia told me she grew up in a strict, rule-oriented, emotionally shut-down environment. She knew her parents loved her; however, their view of family life and Christianity was expressed primarily through intense, smothering control, all of which was securely wrapped in Scripture. She and her sister were forbidden from expressing any challenging emotions. Select verses were misused to prove that emotions were sinful. If she attempted to have an open conversation with her parents to offer her perspective, her counter-opinions were labeled as sinful and disrespectful, which shut down all discourse.

As an adult, Julia experienced high levels of stress if she did something she knew would disappoint her parents, like missing church, having a glass of wine, or disagreeing with them. Driven by a fear of disapproval, she crafted excuses for her decisions, desperate for their validation.

Julia's brain had been wired in conditions where the habituated response to an emotion was to shut it down, where people in authority must not be challenged, where God cares about control more than anything else. She didn't realize her thoughts and actions—the reactive behavior toward her family and her constant need for parents' approval, even as an adult—were habits formed by her brain; they simply felt like the person she was.

The truth is, Julia's habits of emotional regulation (or lack thereof) were formed before she even understood what emotions were. As we worked together, she discovered that she had permission to feel—even the uncomfortable feelings—and that those emotions were not sinful. She learned she had a right to preferences, to be assertive, to have different values from other people. I reminded her regularly that the wiring in her brain had a laid down path of feeling bad when she disappointed others, repressing her emotions, and condemning herself with Bible verses. Over time and with repetition, the new path had become well worn.

Our behavioral and emotional patterns are wired without our explicit permission. We develop habits before we are aware it is happening. These patterns are formed unconsciously by the brain and become well-worn paths.

> ## Our behavioral and emotional patterns are wired without our explicit permission.

Here is a simple and helpful way to envision this brain process of creating new habits. Imagine you are standing in the middle of a large field, with tall wheat growing all around you. When you look to the left, you see a plowed path leading out of the field. Since it is plowed, you assume the path is the best way out. You head that direction to get out of the wheat field; however, it leads to a dilapidated, abandoned shack. That's not where you wanted to end up. The path made it easy to reach, but that ramshackle structure is not where you wanted to go.

You head back to the center of the field and try again. The plowed path—the wrong path—is clearly visible, and you know it would be easy to travel again. But it won't lead you where you want to go. You want to see the beautiful lake that's just on the other side of the field. There's no path cut to the lake, but you have a general idea of the direction you need to go. So, you begin to walk through the wheat in that direction.

It is scratchy and rough. It is hard to know which way to go. There is not a clear direction through, but you keep pushing aside the stalks. Envision how unclear the way forward is and how uncomfortable this feels. One step at a time, you keep pushing aside the stalks. It seems longer than it should be. Finally, you make it out of the field and you end up exactly where you wanted to be. You are scratched up and tired. It was hard. The other path was much easier. But now you see the lake. It is truly beautiful.

Standing in the middle of the field once more, you are confronted with a choice: the well-worn path that leads you astray, or the untamed path leading you towards the lake. When you glance in the direction of the lake, you can't seem to find the path you took. Then you look again, and you see *one* broken stalk of wheat. It's not much of a path, but that one broken stalk is the clue you need. You head that direction. The way is scratchy and uncomfortable. Along the path, you see one other broken stalk, which confirms you are headed in the right direction.

Imagine repeating this scenario over and over, day after day. After dozens and dozens of trips through the new direction in the wheat field, what begins to happen?

A path takes shape.

Sometimes, however, when you are standing in the middle, you turn to walk down the plowed path because it seems like such an easy exit. You instantly regret it. The next day you are back in the middle, and you immediately look toward the lake and ignore the direction of the old path. You now know, without a doubt, that the easier path will not take you where you want to go.

The new path gets clearer every day. You walk a little easier, without tripping. Without getting scratched. The old path also begins to change. Since it is untraveled, new wheat shoots up, making it a little harder to find the clear path down to the shack. You could find your way back down that path without much trouble, but by now, the view of the lake is motivating enough to keep you looking to the new path.

This, my friends, is how the brain creates new habits.

One small step at a time. One moment at a time. One small practice at a time. It is uncomfortable. It is not easy to walk through the field, pushing scratchy stalks out of your way. Most people want to grow but forget that the price of growth is pain. You will trip. You will get up.

> # Most people want to grow but forget that the price of growth is pain.

In her book *Everything is Figureoutable*, Marie Forleo says this about our brain habits: "Yes, permanently changing your neural pathways requires focus, repetition, and dedication. But seriously—can you think of a better use of your time than physically rewiring your brain to help you lead a better life?"

Julia, now in her late forties, recently came back to see me. We reminisced about all the growth she had accomplished in the previous years. She filled me in on how much healthier she relates to her parents and how she has enjoyed growing in her faith without the confines of legalism that had once strangled her.

She told me she wants to develop healthier habits around her tendency to worry. Her teenage daughters are desiring new freedoms, which is increasing her anxiety. She wants to parent with healthy boundaries and stay connected to her girls, without giving in to the old habit of control.

"It looks like you have some new wheat field paths to plow down," I said. "Of course you do. You've never parented teenagers before! Let's start knocking down some stalks, okay?"

3. Your brain is wired for relationship.

In the summers of our kids' growing up years, we were a city-pool family. We beat the Texas heat with the clicking sound of a hole punch on a card-stock swim pass and the screams of giggling kids dunking each other in the water. Madison, Landon, and Colton invited their friends. Yes, with a landline phone call. I tossed snacks in an ice chest, grabbed the swim bag, and off we went.

At that stage of our lives, pool time was not about reading, getting work done, or even relaxing. It was all about playing. I wore durable swimsuits and didn't fuss about freshly washed hair. The kids loved lively games of Sharks and Minnows or Marco Polo, especially if Mom and Dad played along. I spent my fair share of time chasing them in the pool or diving underwater to get the Sharkpedo off the bottom. I am thankful as I reflect that we had no option for screen time on phones or tablets during those years.

Chris and I also spent plenty of time sitting on the edge with our feet dangling in the water, watching them perform crazy tricks off the diving boards. The kids seemed to have an infinite capacity for this. If we happened to look away, they would excitedly yell, "Watch me! Watch me dive! Watch me dive!" In the early years, even a jump was called a dive. They would stand at the end of the board, calling out, "Mom. Mom. Dad. Dad. Watch me. Watch! Watch me dive!" They would dive in, quickly scramble out of the pool, head back to the diving board, starting the whole process over again.

"Watch me dive! Watch me dive! Watch me dive!"

This happened with such frequency, we named the phenomenon and still use the phrase *Watch Me Dive* to describe the deeper process at work. A need much deeper than the dive itself.

Our kids didn't want us to simply watch them dive. They wanted us to watch *them*. They wanted us to be connected. They wanted to be seen. They longed to bring delight. To be enjoyed.

Our kids are well into their adult years now, yet they still have that genuine longing in their souls to be seen. To be known. To be enjoyed.

We all do. Humans are relational beings. We affect each other.

Our brains are literally wired for connection, for closeness. We don't come into the world looking for nice cars or cute clothes. "We come into the world," as Curt Thompson said, "looking for who is looking for us."

Our relational brain is formed by both experience and environment. There is no longer a binary question of nature versus nurture. It is both/and. Relationships are the context in which our brains develop. Because of the mirror neurons in the brain, humans are constantly reading each other, looking for connection and understanding. When relationships are safe, the brain sends a message to calm the stress system, which then creates the environment for the brain's social engagement system to take charge. The social engagement system is the relational brain in action. It is a crucial part of our nervous system, enabling us to connect with others, to be successful in social settings, and to build relationships.

In contrast, when a relationship causes stress, the brain activates its internal threat system and changes the body's chemistry, preparing for fight, flight, or freeze because of the threat.[1] Stress hormones are released in the body, most notably cortisol. The chronic release of stress hormones can significantly disrupt healthy bodily functioning. Research by Dr. John Gottman discovered that highly conflicted couples get sick more frequently than couples with emotionally healthy

---

1   Dr. Stephen Porges's Polyvagal Theory articulates this automated process. He includes the response of *faint* along with fight, flight, and freeze. Some researchers include *fawn*, which can occur as a "tend and befriend" response to abuse. For our purposes, we will simply refer to this process as fight, flight, and freeze.

connections.[2] In one experiment, Gottman's researchers watched how quickly or slowly a scratch would heal. The highly connected couples' scratches healed more quickly. .

When we are closely connected in our families of origin, our brains develop a script for safe relationships. They wire with the full capacity for relational and emotional closeness. When chronic hurt and disconnection are present in those environments, the brain develops altogether differently. Brain scans of abused and neglected children are proof of this.

While trauma is not our primary focus, it is important to address its basic elements, because trauma is deeply rooted in relational experiences. Trauma occurs from a wide variety of stressful situations, most especially from overwhelming and damaging physical, sexual, emotional, environmental, and relational encounters. Those types of experiences impact emotional, physical, and psychosocial development. On the most basic level, when someone is threatened and unsafe and is not provided the resources to be safe, seen, soothed, and secure, trauma responses inevitably emerge to survive the experience. Trauma responses can manifest as chronic hypervigilance; persistent responses of fight, flight, and freeze; emotional dysregulation; physical symptoms; chronic relationship difficulties; and a variety of mental health challenges, such as substance abuse, anxiety disorders, depression, and post-traumatic stress disorder.

When we talk about trauma, it's important to know that trauma responses are not developed *only* because of the circumstance. Any type of suffering is painful, but suffering *all alone* intensifies the effects of trauma.[3] The sense of aloneness is a traumatic experience for the brain, which craves connection. Being in healthy relationships feels good to the brain and body; being disconnected from people is terrifying.

---

2   Drs. John and Julie Gottman founded The Gottman Institute, a research-based approach to relationships. These studies are referenced in the Level One Clinical Foundations in Gottman Method Couples Therapy Training.

3   If you have experienced trauma, remember that you are not alone. Help is available. Reach out to a trusted friend, family member, therapist, or support group.

Mother Teresa, a Catholic nun and missionary who devoted her life to serving the poor and sick in India, knew this well. She said, "Loneliness and the feeling of being unwanted is the most terrible poverty."

Sadly, we live in an extremely lonely time in human history. In 2024, the surgeon general sent out an advisory intended to raise the alarm about the devastating impact of the epidemic of loneliness and isolation in the United States.

An *epidemic* of loneliness and isolation.

Why does all this matter for our soul adventure? Remember, we are wired for connection. This means we are wounded in relationship, and we are healed in relationship. Together, we can heal and be restored; we can find our way back to each other. Together, we can start a revolution of building caring families and connected communities.

> Together, we can start a revolution of building caring families and connected communities.

Michael Cusick was interviewing a neuroscientist on his *Restoring the Soul* podcast and closed out the episode with a question to the guest: "What is one thing people should do over the course of their lives to keep their brains healthy?"

I thought the answer would be something like exercise, get more sleep, eat healthy food, take vitamins, or don't smoke and drink. The list of things we can do to be healthier is endless. I was shocked by his answer: *Never stop building and maintaining healthy relationships.*

Of all the things we can do to keep our brains healthy, positive relationships are at the top of the list.

Yes, we come into the world looking for who is looking for us, and that never changes. The brain, body, and soul are designed for connection. Let's keep the Watch-Me-Dive phenomenon alive and well, okay? Our relational brains need each other.

4. Your brain is focused on survival.

Our home is in the forest, nestled in Texas's beautiful Piney Woods. A tree canopy covers our home. Along with the beauty come the beasts. Our little neck of the woods has snakes and scorpions, armadillos and ants, wild hogs and woodpeckers, raccoons and rabbits. Don't even get me started on the deer.

I have learned to be careful when I'm outside. I'm especially mindful of creatures that sting and bite. Getting stung once by a scorpion was enough to keep me vigilant. And my sturdy fear of snakes, which developed after my mom was bitten by a copperhead when I was growing up, has served me well.

Remember the story about my high jump over a copperhead? It's time for part two.

A couple weeks after I heroically avoided the coiled snake on the street, I was raking leaves in the yard. Suddenly, I jumped up and over to the side, throwing the rake in the air. Just like when I was on the street, I had no idea why I jumped. I looked all around in the grass. Then I saw it. On the ground beside my rake was a wavy, copper-colored stick, rounded on both ends. A *stick*.

Not a snake.

Copperheads can be tricky to identify in our area where twigs and leaves match their natural camouflage. Jumping from a stick that *looked* like a snake was the survival function of my brain working in full force.

My brain was doing what it perceived as necessary to keep me safe. The survival function took command of my brain and body when I jumped both times. One time it sent messages for me to jump when there was a snake, another time it sent messages to me to jump when there was *not* a snake. My jumps were not decisions on the part of my conscious self.

Your brain is focused on survival. It is designed to work to keep you alive in this big, scary world. The same survival function that kept humans safe from wooly mammoths and saber-toothed tigers is still keeping us safe in our modern world. The challenge for this part of our brain is that dangers in the modern world are not as clear cut as the threats that our ancestors faced.

The survival brain is built for rapid response. It quickly sorts all stimuli into one of two categories, good or bad. It doesn't work with nuance. To speed the sorting process and reaction time, the brain remains on high alert for *possible* danger. The brain does not need to be 100 percent sure there is a real danger in order to activate the threat response system.

The appearance of something that looked like a snake was enough to kick my survival brain into high gear. Earlier, I mentioned the automated responses of fight, flight, and freeze. Well, I literally took flight at the sight of a stick.

The brain's survival instinct is to self-protect. Those fast reactions can show up in the way we function in our everyday lives. The survival system triggers hormonal and psychological changes before our conscious brain has a chance to respond.

Those split-second responses are activated in the amygdala (part of the limbic system), whereas our reasoning skills occur in the prefrontal cortex (PFC). The PFC is the most advanced part of the brain and is where executive brain functioning occurs. When we are using our fully integrated brain, the PFC is relationally connected, can solve problems, regulate emotions, is flexible, focused, controls impulsivity, and activates working memory. In terms of neural firing time, the processes that take place in the PFC are incredibly slow in comparison to the automated survival processes in the brain.

Fight, flight, and freeze get activated at the first sign of threat, while the conscious, rational PFC is still considering all the information and weighing its options.

Case in point: I was driving on the freeway when a car pulled right up on my bumper. I yelled into the rearview mirror, "You better back off, dude!" He didn't. I sped up and yelled again, "You *better* back off!" (I won't type what I really said. Can I blame Arneckeville?)

In the protection of my car, flight wasn't my survival brain's go-to response; fight was. One final time I screamed at the mirror, "I SAID BACK OFF!"

Then, with nothing but raw anger running the show, I slammed on my brakes. I was going to teach him a thing or two about tailgating!

Now let's pause a moment to ask a few rational, PFC-type questions: To whom was I going to teach a thing or two? Him? Really? How on earth was that going to work?

My survival brain's fight reaction almost caused him to crash into my bumper at seventy-five miles per hour. Not my best moment. But a perfect, if embarrassing, example of how quickly the survival brain works. Or in this case, *doesn't*.

The Integrated Brain

Your brain is, indeed, amazing. It's complex and intricately designed. At its best, it can grow and change, empower you to form new habits, allow you to find and develop mutually beneficial connections with others, and keep you alive to traverse this earth one more day.

Moments like my episode on the highway demonstrate why we need our *integrated brain*. The root of integrated is *integrate*, meaning whole. When the brain is integrated, all the differentiated parts are working together. Problems arise when we move through situations without the benefit of our whole, integrated brain.

By neglecting mindfulness and self-regulation strategies, we rely on autopilot—a setting that runs primarily on habit and fear. We simply react, like I did when I slammed on my brakes in the middle of the freeway. In those moments, we're not thinking with our whole brain, but one tiny, important but primitive part of it.

You know what I mean, right? Those moments when you lose your cool, say something you regret, or do something foolish and impulsive in the heat of the moment. Snapping at your child for singing the same song over and over. Screaming at a traffic light. Barking at the computer because the internet is slow. Yelling at your husband for chewing loudly. (You're laughing, but I know I'm not the only one.)

In those moments, it's as if we lose control of our mental faculties. Rational thought and reasoning go offline, and the result is explosive, mysterious, and downright scary. To be clear, I'm not referring to the mental state of psychosis or the diagnosable and very real mental health illnesses like schizophrenia or bipolar disorder, but about everyday lapses of losing control. Those moments when we feel trapped in a state of numbness or reactivity—fight, flight, freeze. We need our integrated brain online to help us navigate our lives in a healthy way.

Let's talk about a user-friendly way to make sense of this. Dr. Dan Siegal's hand model of the brain offers a simple illustration, demonstrating what he calls the upstairs and downstairs brain.

Put your thumb in the middle of your palm and then curl your fingers over the top. In this illustration, the top of your hand is the cortex, and your fingernails represent the thinking PFC brain: the upstairs brain.

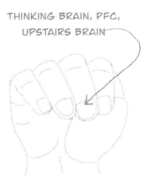

THINKING BRAIN, PFC,
UPSTAIRS BRAIN

When you lift your fingers, your thumb symbolizes the limbic system, the fear center. This, along with your palm and wrist, represent the downstairs brain. The limbic system serves many functions, but for this simple illustration, our focus is on one small part, the amygdala, which we learned about earlier.

AMYGDALA,
FEAR CENTER,
DOWNSTAIRS BRAIN

If you pull your fingers back over the top of your thumb, we are looking again at the upstairs brain, the calm relational brain. When the amygdala fires an alert of possible danger, the PFC goes offline, flipping the lid up. To demonstrate, flip your four fingers up, leaving your thumb over your palm. This "danger" alert fires more easily when you are hungry, tired, stressed, or if someone or a situation is pushing one of your emotional buttons. Traumatic experiences can sensitize the reactivity in the limbic system, causing even minor stressors to flip your lid and shove the PFC off-line.

When that happens, you've lost all that the PFC provides: flexibility and emotional balance, reasoning skills, empathy, your values, and insight. Without access to your PFC, you can act in ways that can be dangerous or frightening to others. The downstairs brain is in charge, the upstairs brain is offline.

I flipped my lid when the tailgater pushed an emotional button for me. Truth be told, I am a very competitive driver. When someone passes me, I feel like I've lost a competition. I'm the one who never wanted to pull over on family road trips for bathroom breaks for the kids. I didn't want all those people I passed to win the race. I know. It's bad.

My limbic system fired from the emotion of anger, to which I am highly sensitized. What logical sense did it make for me to hit my

CALM RELATIONAL
BRAIN

OFFLINE OR FLIPPED LID

brakes while speeding on the freeway, a car directly behind me? Why didn't I simply change lanes?

It made zero sense! None. *Nada.*

That's what happens when the amygdala—primal instinct—runs the show. With my lid flipped, my logical brain was not available to me at that moment.

The question is, why? Generally speaking, I'm a rational, thoughtful person. Most of the time. So why did the irrational, reactive part of my brain take control?

My attention.

I paid more attention to the driver's behavior than to my own body's warning signs, which caused the situation to escalate. If I had gently focused on my body's changes, I would have noticed the tightness in my chest, increased heart rate, hands gripping the steering wheel, eyes darting quickly back and forth between the rearview and side mirrors. (See the Appendix for strategies to calm your body after your lid flips.)

Had I noticed and heeded those signals, I would have been able to breathe, focus my attention elsewhere, practice mindfulness strategies, move over a lane, and let the impatient driver go on his stupid, merry way.

One more thing: Have you ever wondered why you get really upset by things that don't seem to upset other people? Chris responds the exact opposite of me. He would *never* care in a hundred bazillion years about a tailgating driver. He would immediately put on his blinker, move over a lane, smile and wave ever so kindly, and keep whistling *Walking on Sunshine* while his blinker stays on for the next five miles.

I'll tell you why that happens in the section about packing your story. Be on the lookout for one small, but crucial bit of information you need to know about your amygdala.

Now, let's keep packing.

Do the Work

What relationship needs your attention today? Name the person you want to reach out to and what you specifically want to do differently. Make a plan for when and how you will do it.

Do the Joy

Joy brings energy to the body! Name three small activities that bring you joy. Pick one and do it today.

YOUR STORY

It takes enormous trust and courage to allow
yourself to remember.

—— BESSEL VAN DER KOLK ——

Teresa and Jimmy sat together on the couch without touching. Silence echoed off the walls of the enormous, invisible chasm between them. Teresa crossed her arms as she rigidly turned away from Jimmy. Her jaw tightly clenched, she stared over at the books on my desk. Jimmy looked at her, attempting to coax her to look back at him. She refused to budge. Tightening his lips, he shook his head in discouragement. The air was thick with pain.

We had been attempting to uncover the cause of their disconnection. The more they described their frustrations, the more tension filled the space. Neither of them was getting what they needed from the other. He felt anxious about their relationship. She felt smothered. He felt unsettled when she had a bad day. She felt annoyed by his constant checking in with her. He felt last on her to-do list, while she insisted he was too needy.

Looking Back to Move Forward

Teresa and Jimmy needed to explore their original stories of hurt and loss if they were ever going to understand the moves in this dance of disconnection. Their pasts were affecting their present. If we didn't get to the root of their issues, they might not have a future. But I knew they wouldn't like the line of questioning necessary to get us there:

What did comfort look like for you as a child?

Tell me about how your parents handled conflict.

Was it safe to let your parents know something bothered you? What would you do to let them know?

What did you learn from your family about emotions and vulnerability?

Couples' therapy too often settles for teaching better communication and listening skills and fails to dig deeper to root out the source of the disconnection.

It does no good to cut the top off the dandelion without digging up the root.

In the previous chapter, we learned that the brain is wired for relationship. From infancy on, we look for the people who are looking for us. What happens, then, to the children who look, only to find that no one is looking for them? What happens if that child was hurt, scared, ignored, bullied? Curt Thompson says, "We can grow up in homes in which the food finds the table, the money finds the college funds, and the family even finds the church each Sunday; but somehow our hearts remain undiscovered by the two people we most need to know us—our parents."

Our patterns of relating are held in our bodies and in the way we move in our relationships. These patterns form in our earliest relationships, and we often follow them for the rest of our lives. Most of us rarely consider how our early hurts and experiences shape who we are today.

What stories did Teresa and Jimmy hold in their bodies that contributed to the way they move in their relational patterns?

Like most people, Teresa and Jimmy wanted relief in the here and now. They wanted someone to help them fix the pain. There is nothing wrong with wanting relief; however, another paradox of soul adventuring is that we need to enter pain to find relief.

We must look back to see the way forward.

> # We must look back to see the way forward.

Ignoring or covering up our past may make us temporarily feel better, but the adage "we are only as sick as our secrets" turns out to be true. Researchers have discovered that our bodies feel stressed when we hold back the truth. As neuroscientist David Eagleman explains, "Your brain doesn't like to keep secrets." When you are minimizing your past, the part of your brain that wants to tell the truth is constantly fighting with the part of your brain that wants to keep the information hidden. The conflict floods the body with stress hormones.

Healing begins when we are honest with ourselves. Undoubtedly, some truths are hard to face. Telling ourselves the truth about our stories requires bravery. What Teresa and Jimmy discovered—and what I hope you will, too—is that the truth brings freedom and joy as we learn to remake our relational habits. This is what makes your story the next piece of essential gear to pack for your soul adventure.

Once Upon a Time

Suffering is the linchpin of all stories, holding together every great narrative. Look how this works.

Once upon a time, there was a girl named Dorothy who lost both of her parents and lived with her Auntie Em and her dog, Toto.

Once upon a time, there was a boy named Luke Skywalker who didn't know who his father was.

Once upon a time, there was a boy named Harry who had a scar on his forehead and lived in a room underneath a stairwell in the house of his awful Aunt Petunia and Uncle Vernon.

Do you see the connection? In each of these stories, the protagonist faces challenges, overcomes obstacles, and fights against enemies. What draws us into those stories is the conflict. Even if our own stories are wildly different (it's hard to compete with tornados, starfighters, and magic), we engage emotionally with those tales because, on some level, we relate to the character's pain.

It's easy to see how those famous characters were affected by their pasts. Their stories are written out for us. We know their tales from beginning to end.

But what about your story?

To know your story is to know yourself. You can't change what you are not aware of. Conversely, the ripple effect of knowing your story travels through all the relationships in your life.

All our stories began with a *once upon a time*. In that moment, a precious event started a new story. One new life entered the world and, by the very essence of birth, changed history. The world changed the moment you were born.

> ## To know your story is to know yourself.

In the Beginning

I would argue that knowing your story starts with understanding the *first* story: the story of God and his creation. It begins with God doing what he does best: creating and delighting, over and over, through sky, sea, landscapes, and creatures of all shapes and sizes.

The apex of this story is God's most wonderful creation: the creation of humankind. Humans made in his image, made for relationship, made to be connected to God and each other. There is delight, beauty, and nakedness with no shame. We don't have a tremendous amount of narrative letting us know what this was like, but Scripture tells us that the garden is where all things were perfect.

God looked at everything he had created and saw that it was good. The Hebrew word used here, *tov*, implies that God saw his creation as more than just functionally good. *Tov* alludes to something being aesthetically pleasing. God delighted in what he created.

Conflict shows up in this story in Genesis 3; this conflict is referred to as *the fall.* Brokenness entered the world. Broken trust. Broken relationships. Broken hearts.

The story names a serpent as the true villain behind the disruption. The book of Revelation names the serpent as "that ancient serpent called the devil, or Satan, who leads the whole world astray" (Revelation 12:9, NIV).

The cunning serpent struck with a lie that created division between the key players in the story. He understood that relational separation and, worse, isolation, are a recipe for disaster in the human experience. Adam and Eve were instantly separated from God, which disrupted every relationship in the garden. No longer a place of perfect unity and peace, creation had been infected with sin, shame, blame, and brokenness.

Later, God walks into the scene and asks, "Where are you?" The question is not about Adam and Eve's physical location but their emotional and spiritual connection. God created humanity with relationship in mind, and the rest of the story is about him working to reconnect and restore the broken relationship.

God is always looking to find you, not looking to condemn you. He wants you to know his eyes are searching for you in your mess and brokenness. He loves you. Unconditionally. God's desire and good plan is for you to live in relational joy and connection with him and others.

> ## God is always looking to find you, not looking to condemn you.

Knowing the first story validates your story. We are all longing for connection; we were created for it! But we were born into a world of brokenness and loss. That reality means that no matter how great your parents were, none of us got everything we needed in childhood. Certainly, not all our stories are traumatic. Some of them are full of beauty and deep relational connection; however, we all have hard elements in our stories. It's naïve to say, "Oh well, none of us got what we needed. My life wasn't really that bad." I am inviting you to acknowledge the truth of your story—all of it. Because the hurts and losses you have experienced along the way affect the way you relate in the here and now.

The road ahead is treacherous and beautiful.

Chris and I have seen some awe-inspiring views on our travels, and it seems like the most beautiful views happened on the most terrifying roads. When we stopped at the south entrance of Sequoia National Park, a ranger warned us the narrow, windy road through the park would be a challenge for us to drive due to the combined length of our truck and camper. This was hard to believe, because let me tell you, we own one of the *tiniest* of campers possible. It's a fun-size camper! It is a compact, vintage teardrop, less than ten feet long, end to end.

We decided he knew better than us. We turned around to leave the park, quickly adjusting Google Maps to reroute us to the north entrance. Chris was driving, leaving me as navigator. As soon as we exited the park, the map showed a road running parallel to the park entrance, a little to the west. It looked like a shorter route than driving all the way back to the freeway. "Here! Turn here!" I spouted. "Take this road!"

Remember, I lean to the impulsive side.

Chris quickly turned onto the road. From the moment we set out, we knew we were in for a tense, white-knuckled drive. I had unknowingly picked a route far more treacherous than the park road, and there was no way to turn around. The road we took made the original Sequoia road look like a four-lane freeway. For most of the drive, it was a one-lane, cliffs on one side, sheer drop-offs on the other, and loads of hairpin turns, tires only inches from the edge. Chris fiercely gripped the steering wheel while I grasped the door handles with sweaty palms and a dry mouth.

Let me tell you, we would have preferred an easier way, but there was no changing it. That challenging road delivered stunning views. The drive was simultaneously scary and breathtaking.

It is the same with entering your stories, your own roads of hurt, loss, betrayal. The rugged path where your pain lands in the road right in front of you.

We own our stories so we don't spend our lives denying them or being defined by them.

Your Story Shapes Your Brain

Your brain's limbic system (your thumb-in-the-hand model) is where memories and emotions are stored. This tiny area of your brain is saturated with experiences, and it has a long memory. Within the limbic system, your amygdala serves as the fear and emotional sensor for the brain. We are born with a fully functioning amygdala. From birth on, the limbic system has been storing information about what is safe and what is not safe, who is available and who is not available. Your neural networks wired and fired according to all those early experiences.

Here's one example of how this wiring and firing works: If yelling, violence, and chaos are the normal way of relating in a home, the amygdala senses a lack of safety. The threat system turns off the social engagement system and activates the stress system, which releases stress hormones. Children need comfort. They need someone who is aware and mindfully tuned in to their stressful and overwhelming experiences.

This is called attunement. Without it, the relational pattern created can be one of social *dis*engagement, where children conclude they must navigate the stressful experience alone. It's a pattern that, like the well-worn path through the wheat field, gets traveled again and again. Without intentional interruption, the seeds that were sown will grow into relational patterns based on those early experiences.

Each of us carries implicit memories like these. They are forged deeply in our emotional memory bank, activating thoughts, beliefs, and emotions central to how we see ourselves.

At its core, story work is relationship work. Knowing your story equips you to identify and understand the relational patterns, scripts, traditions, values, and blessings in your life that you want to stop, start, and continue. As you deepen your understanding of what shaped you, you gain the power to change it.

As you seek to understand your story, I invite you to be intentional about your approach. When my clients have maladaptive coping skills, they tend to believe they are broken and in need of fixing. In truth, they are wounded and in need of healing. The appropriate question needs to be "What happened to me?" as opposed to "What's wrong with me?"

Asking *what happened* is about gaining self-awareness and insight to understand the relational patterns that formed. As the saying goes, *hurt people hurt people*, but understanding your story empowers you to see the path to developing healthier relationships as you address unresolved emotional issues.

As I said earlier, you can't change what you are not aware of. Becoming aware of our stories—acknowledging the truth—is what allows us to break the generational cycles of addiction, codependency, mental health struggles, and abuse.[4]

---

4 Abuse is multifaceted, including emotional, physical, sexual, financial, psychological, or spiritual harm and exploitation.

Fact Finding, Not Fault Finding

Uncovering our origin stories is about fact-finding. This is not a fault-finding mission. I'm not the conductor of the blame-your-family train, begging all of you to come aboard. Blame has been around since the infamous scene in Genesis 3, where everyone in the story (except God) points their finger at someone else. Blame doesn't heal; it only adds to the hurt.

Ben and I had been working to make sense of the severe depression he felt trapped in. A heavy blanket of sadness weighed on him, depleting his energy resources and leaving him unmotivated and paralyzed with self-contempt. In a span of only two years, he had experienced the loss of both of his parents, a farming accident that left him with physical and emotional scars, and the birth of a child with mild disabilities. After several sessions of talk therapy, we applied the trauma-informed EMDR protocol.

Men with tears on their faces always render me silent.

The former college baseball player sat quietly on my couch, his cheeks wet with tears. Silent sobs softened his muscular frame. Finally, he spoke, "I guess I *have* had hard things happen to me. I suppose I never really gave myself permission to call them hard."

Recognizing that the real question was "What happened to me?" instead of "What's wrong with me?" He finally understood that he was not finding fault or blaming but facing the facts of his past. Through time in sessions, he was able to move away from the self-blame that had been haunting him and coloring his story with depression.

Attachment Stories

Once upon a time, a mom was afraid to face her sorrow.

A crushing sadness landed on my chest as I stared blankly out of the kitchen bay window into the greenbelt behind our house. Snapping my attention back to the table where I sat reading my Developmental Psychology textbook, I wondered at the heaviness that had appeared out of nowhere. With furrowed brows, I glared at the book, realizing the words on the page were the source of the emotion.

I was working on my master's degree, finishing homework while the kids were at school. It was a typical clumsy textbook with too many words and too few pictures to be much fun. I'm a reading scanner, gifted with the ability to quickly find what might be on a quiz. I flipped to the chapter on John Bowlby and Mary Ainsworth's research exploring childhood attachment patterns, casually reading about the different attachment styles.[5] Rereading the section on avoidant attachment, I reflected on conflicts I had been having with our teenage kids. The more I read, the more uncomfortable I felt. The casualness of the moment was gone; the air in the room turned ominous. The page screamed a truth I hadn't considered.

Why were my eyes brimming with tears? Where did this sadness come from? Why did the ache seem laced with a toxic dose of shame? I slammed the book shut, got up, and walked away.

I've always been proud of my independence. Being self-sufficient and confident are qualities I value deeply. Figuring out my own stuff and blazing through life is a high priority for me. I love people; don't get me wrong. My friends from every life stage are living proof of this value. I've always been the girl with a group gathered around, telling one of my tall tales or admitting one of my silly life blunders. I love them, but I don't want to *need* them.

I *hate* feeling needy. I am unskilled at letting people know when I am in need, in real time. Reaching out vulnerably for comfort is foreign. When I feel needy, I feel weak.

Truth be told, the kids entering the teenage years had been hard for me emotionally. My heart yearned for emotional connection, yet the best I could muster was head-hanging shame after an angry outburst. This longing scared and confused me, like an invisible barrier I couldn't quite name. My friends would tell me of their late-night, heart-to-heart

---

5   John Bowlby and Mary Ainsworth's research, known as "Attachment Theory," focused on exploring how early interactions between infants and their primary caregivers shape emotional bonds and attachment styles.

chats with their daughters. It seemed like I didn't know how to do that. I felt locked out of the kids' hearts during those years; a tall stone fortress guarded my emotional world.

Surely, I thought, *if I go on a run or plan a trip, I'll be able to escape the weight of this massive, dark sadness.* As an Enneagram seven and devoted fun seeker, I'll do almost anything on the planet to keep myself from facing the hard stuff. But I wanted to be open emotionally, to feel more deeply. To do that, I had to face the truth of my story.

I can tell you from experience, not just head knowledge, that story work is worth the risk.

Attachment Theory 101

Attachment theory is the study of lasting psychological connectedness between human beings. The central theme of attachment theory is that when a child's primary caregivers are available and responsive to an infant's needs, the child develops a sense of security. With the security of a dependable caregiver, the child feels safe to explore the world. The converse is also true. A child will develop with a sense of insecurity if the primary caregivers are unavailable or undependable physically or emotionally. Our childhood experiences, both positive and negative, profoundly shape our beliefs about love and how to give and receive it.

Thus, the two main types of attachment are secure and insecure. Researchers have identified three subsets of insecure attachment: avoidant (dismissive), anxious (preoccupied), and disorganized (fearful-avoidant.)

Our stories and attachment types matter because they explain the way we interact with others throughout our lives. We are made to be seen, heard, and felt by someone who desires to see us, hear us, and feel what we feel. Remember: Story work is relational work.

We all come into the adult world with patterns already established in our soul, patterns we are often unaware of. Those patterns can keep us exhausted, alone, and confused. The goal of soul adventuring is to live healthier, wholehearted lives. Gaining insight about stories, attachment types, and relational patterns empowers us to reorient ourselves and move in a purposeful direction—a direction we *want* to go.

Below, I've included statements that represent how someone of each type might feel, think, and behave as well as a brief overview of each attachment type. As you read about each attachment type, ponder your relational history. Notice the basic ways you function in your relationships, both past and present. In the Appendix, you will find a set of questions to help you explore your story and attachment style.

Secure

I feel safe asking for my needs to be met and trusting I can meet yours as well. I am able to give and receive comfort.

Securely attached people can adequately and frequently express vulnerable emotions while regulating self and are able to listen to other's emotions and needs without overreacting. The primary words of secure attachment are safe, seen, soothed, secure.

Insecure: Avoidant

I don't need you. I'm fine. I've got me, why would I need anyone else? I value independence so don't ask too much of me.

The avoidant style is overly committed to independence and struggles with intimacy and vulnerability. They tend to respond to stress by moving away from the other, retreating into other activities to distract themselves.

Insecure: Anxious

Wait, why are you backing away? Stop pulling away from me. Don't leave me. I need more from you. I'm afraid you're leaving me. Don't abandon me!

The anxious style wants intimacy but fears rejection and often gets clingy and needy. They tend to respond to relationship stress by anxiously moving toward the other for more connection or validation.

Insecure: Disorganized

Come close to me! Draw near to me. Never mind, I'm going to subconsciously sabotage and make you go away. Never mind! I want you back. No, I don't. I'm going to run for my life. Now I want you. Never mind, I'll sabotage it again.

Those with the disorganized style crave intimacy but distrust people and end up pushing them away in a constant battle of a come close/go away pattern.

Back to our once-upon-a-time beginning and my story, the mom who was afraid to face her sorrow. That same mom who slammed the textbook shut opened her heart to exploration.

Little by little, I have grown in my resilience to face how my attachment wounds were formed. As my willingness to understand my own attachment pattern has expanded, so has my ability to change it and walk in new ways. That's the beauty of having a brain that can change and form new habits.

God built our brain with the ability to develop new, healthy attachments! I went to therapy, learned more about attachment research from the pioneers in the field, and worked on my attachment with my husband. I also studied Scripture, prayed, and read books by Christian authors who recognize the intersection of theology and interpersonal neurobiology. All of this guided me in understanding how to repair my attachment to both God and others.

Sadness continues to show up when I read about attachment, but it doesn't feel as heavy as before. It's what I would call a timeline longing, me standing here in this moment, reaching back toward the younger Christine on an earlier spot on the timeline, wishing I could help her understand more about herself when she had littles.

I am a gracious time-traveler to that younger Christine. She was doing a pretty good job; gosh, she was most certainly a fun mom. But I also feel sad for how detached she was from herself and others.

Do you feel those kinds of longings? A wish that you could have done things a little differently? My hunch is you *do* have those longings, just like me. We have all made mistakes; there is no other way through life. I want to say this: Don't give up. Soul adventuring is about hope. It's about the belief that it is *never* too late to change.

I am proud of myself for listening to my hunger for deeper relationships, facing my story, and learning how to attach and connect in healthier ways.

I practiced showing up for each of our kids with a more solid, secure attachment. My time at family gatherings shifted as I listened and shared with a new openness instead of hiding behind funny stories. In doing so, I made room for more vulnerable emotions. When the opportunity presented itself, I took responsibility for ways I hurt my children due to my lack of attunement and poor emotional skills in their early years. Today, I treasure the tender closeness I feel with them and each of their significant others.

During Madison's wedding planning season, we giggled and chatted, dreaming of how to make her wedding day magical. (It was, by the way! It even had a jumping booth!). During Covid, I slipped past hospital security to sneak into the room to get one quick glimpse of my brave girl holding her first baby girl. I helped with the middle of the night feedings after each of the girls were born, tiptoeing into her room with Nora and then Ivey, waking her with a soft touch on the arm and then passing her a swaddled bundle of joy to nurse. She is the gentlest and sweetest of mothers. My heart swoons when I watch her love on her girls.

Landon doesn't leave our home to head back to his apartment without plopping down on the couch to chat. He excitedly checks in with me, always full of questions about how my therapy office is running, my next speaking or writing gig, or simply about how things are going in our lives. He shares lively details about his latest Dungeons and Dragons campaign or a recent friend gathering he organized or fills me in on the highs and lows he is experiencing in his life. He loves bringing his gang of friends to our house, showing off our backyard haven and enjoying lively conversations and a steak meal around our dinner table.

Colton and I have shared a cherished, sweet rhythm since his high school days, sitting side by side on the barstools in the kitchen, shooting the breeze or untangling an intense friendship dilemma and every single thing in between. During the mother/son dance at his wedding, my tears flowed without restraint. We danced nose to nose under the high, vaulted ceilings of the gorgeous barn venue, Michael Bublé's smooth, velvety voice filling the room with promises to love forever. When I wasn't crying, we chatted like we were sitting on those two bar stools in the kitchen. The moment was eternal and sacred, the shared tenderness of our mother-son relationship on full display.

Turns out, that slammed-shut textbook was a wide-open portal, a pathway to new bravery and joy. Our family life is not perfect, of course. We are a work in progress. But doing the work feels a lot like joy.

Now, it's your turn. Understanding your story is essential to your soul adventure.

Do the work. Do the joy. I promise, your soul adventuring will be worth every single switchback and terrifying turn.

Do the Work

What is one unhealthy pattern in your life that you learned from your family of origin? Talk to a friend about how you can respond in healthier ways. Ask God to give you wisdom to build healthier ways of relating.

Do the Joy

Reflect on a relationship that has brought you joy in your life. Write two or three sentences of gratitude for this relationship.

– 6 –
YOUR EMOTIONAL WORLD

Despite our fear, there is something in us that
wants to feel all these emotional energies,
because they are the juice of life.

MIRIAM GREENSPAN

Chris and I plopped down uncomfortably on the sagging couch
in the marriage therapist's office. While the well-worn seating might have been less than ideal, our discomfort stemmed
primarily from the reality that after years of helping other couples, we
now found ourselves in the position of needing help.

The transition to parenting adolescents had stirred up a sea of conflict in our once-tranquil marriage. More to the point, parenting teens
was tying this wild and free-spirited, adventurous girl into an anxious
knot. The fun-loving, playful mom I once had been was exiled to a
faraway land, replaced by someone neither Chris nor I recognized.

The cause of my turmoil? Our sweet children were mutating into sneaky, rebellious teens. Worse, they were morphing into sneaky, rebellious creatures who *were just like me*. Like cute, awkward little apples, they were falling on the ground beside their mama's wild-and-free apple tree.

I was bound and determined to chore-chart the *me* out of them, preach the *me* out of them, memory verse the *me* out of them.

Why? Because the stories my high school besties, Pam and Tara, and I can tell–without stretching the truth–would make any parent shake their head in disbelief. As much as I giggle with Pam and Tara about our Cuero High School days, I wanted our kids to make healthier choices than I had made. Those funny stories from my past included some real-life consequences. Heck, I had two car wrecks *before* I was sixteen!

Can you see why I was a little freaked out?

To be fair, my parents tried their best, but I was pretty sneaky. And rebellious.

Full of worry, suspicion, and no small amount of shame, I longed to help our kids navigate their adolescent years with a wee bit more wisdom and discernment than I'd had.

Parenting teenagers was a crash course in facing my own emotions. I felt out of control. Fear ran rampant in my worst-case-scenario brain.

Turns out, their teenage years had way more to do with what God was teaching me about me than what God was teaching them.

My emotional turmoil left Chris dazed and confused. *Who kidnapped his fun-loving bride and replaced her with this crazed Christine?* He had become accustomed to the easy-breezy ways of the Christine he had lived with during our first seventeen years of marriage. The anxiety was making me rigid, convincing me there was only *one* right answer to each parenting dilemma we faced. We were polarized in our responses: I was becoming dogmatic; he was becoming passive.

Gridlock had us in its grips. Like any therapist worth their salt, our counselor tapped into our childhood stories to uncover the origins of our conflicts, learning how they led to the maze of disconnection in which we were trapped. Most importantly, he invited us to explore our emotional worlds and discover how our stories and current experiences collided to trigger deep emotional responses within us.

I worked on being less activated by anxiety. I named my emotions and tried to be less critical of Chris's parenting style. Chris focused on understanding his emotions, naming his deep need to please. He willingly practiced facing conflict in a healthier manner. With time and patience, we learned how to show up for ourselves and each other in new ways.

Two Words That Changed My Life

During one session, as Chris and I sat on that saggy couch, a brief exchange with our therapist changed my life.

> **Me:** (In a cheerful, bragging voice) I've done so much better this week. I've not said a word to Chris every time I thought he was wrong! I definitely disagreed with his parenting choices, but I said nothing. I'm so proud of myself.
>
> **Chris:** (Long blinks. Lips tight. Both eyebrows raised.)
>
> **Therapist:** (A true master at his craft, he allowed silence to do its piercing work. He slowly looked at Chris, then back at me.)
>
> **Me:** (Annoyed, looking at Chris and those stupid eyebrows. I looked back at our therapist, blurting out in a strong burst of defensiveness.) Wait a second! I said *nothing* to him about how mad I was when he was wrong! That's good, right?
>
> **Therapist:** (Slowly, gently looking at each of us.) Christine, I believe you. You did great to restrain from verbally criticizing him. But what you *felt* about Chris is still very evident. It leaks.

Two tiny words. *It leaks.* Tiny, yet bold enough to fill the room. They echoed in the room and in my mind as if bouncing off canyon walls.

In that moment, I realized that although I had made strides in my emotional work, the sheer speed and power of my unnamed emotions continued to cause challenges in our relationship. Seeping out without my noticing. Affecting others in ways I hadn't intended. Clearly, I had more work to do.

Our emotional world is present with us, whether we acknowledge it or not.

It leaks.

No one can escape this reality. Eduardo Bericat, a sociology professor at the University of Seville, says, "As human beings we can only experience life emotionally." There is no other way.

Make some room in that suitcase, friend. It's time to pack the third crucial piece of gear for your soul adventure: *your emotional world.*

Be careful, it leaks.

On that day almost twenty years ago, when Chris and I plopped onto that saggy couch, my emotions were leaking, yet I felt powerless to do anything about it. I was in my early forties and realizing for the first time that I did not know how to face sadness, disappointment, loneliness, or uncertainty. Because I couldn't face my own emotions, I lacked the skills to help our kids face theirs. My emotional reactivity showed up in numerous ways:

- My anger seemed to be caused by *their* behavior. I wrongly believed my anger was their fault.
- My fear consumed me. Trying to control Chris's parenting behavior was my feeble attempt to quell the chaotic fear inside me.
- My walls were up. If a friend expressed disappointment or was upset, I reacted defensively.

That younger Christine was blind to the swirling emotions inside of her, which led her to try her best to control other's emotions in order to control *something*. Her rage, blame, and defensiveness showed up without permission. Once again, I have a lot of grace for that younger Christine. She was doing the best she could but most certainly needed to learn better so she could do better.

Now I understand how my early experiences shaped my behavior. The emotional modeling I received was restricted and failed to equip me to regulate my emotions.

It's impossible to do something you have never learned. So yes, I do have compassion for myself.

However, my limited emotional expression and reactivity caused relational distance and shame. How could it not? Fun and playful one minute, then fearful and angry the next, I wasn't emotionally safe. This is not something I admit to easily. I desperately wanted to be emotionally close to the people in my life, but I didn't know how.

On that therapist's couch, I learned for the first time how to let myself feel and face my disappointment and sadness. I entered my own story of hurt and loss, which illuminated why I was desperately attempting to control the kids. I was attempting to heal my story by controlling theirs. It doesn't work like that.

As I named my challenging emotions, I built my capacity to be with the kids when they had their own difficult emotions. I learned how to listen without reacting or trying to fix their problems. I made many mistakes and still do.

It takes time.

> I was attempting to heal my story by controlling theirs. It doesn't work like that.

Most of us are poorly trained in how to navigate our emotional world. Many of my clients used the word *emotional* as a derogatory name for themselves when they talk about times when they've felt overly sad or angry. Others describe their numbness to life by saying, "I'm not emotional, and I just go with the flow."

Emotions have gotten a bad rap, especially in the Christian world, where the majority of discipleship tends to focus on keeping feelings tightly contained while relying solely on logic and truth. We lose touch with ourselves when we do this. Integrating the emotional world *into* the rational world is the wellspring of our deepest wisdom. Without the ability to access our emotional world and regulate our emotions, we are incapable of functioning at our highest levels intellectually or relationally.

> Integrating the emotional world *into* the rational world is the wellspring of our deepest wisdom.

The American Psychological Association defines emotional maturity as a high and appropriate level of emotional control and expression. The definition of emotional immaturity is a tendency to express emotions without restraint or disproportionately to the situation. Those definitions will be the trail map for how we move through this section, but I want to note a distinction. I prefer the word *regulate* rather than control when we're talking about emotions. Remember that we can only experience the world emotionally. We can't control that we feel, but we can regulate our response to our feelings.

Pressure Cookers and Beach Balls

At its most basic level, emotion is energy. Energy is powerful. It can do so much good! Suppressed energy, however, can cause a lot of damage.

Let's use steam as an example. I have vivid childhood memories of my mom cooking with the old-style pressure cookers. I don't know if you have ever been around one of those intimidating pieces of cookware, but they were a little on the scary side. You are probably familiar with the InstaPot, today's more modern electric pressure cookers. An InstaPot is like a gentle butterfly compared to the caterpillar version of the pressure cookers of the 1970s.

Those old cookers were heavy. They had a bulky lid that locked into place to create a tight seal, trapping the steam inside. A weighted safety valve on the lid jiggled when the pressure was high enough, releasing excess steam to prevent the cooker from exploding. The heat and pressure of the expanding steam quickly cooked whatever food you'd locked inside the pot. The powerful energy trapped inside that pressure cooker could also do some serious damage if it wasn't handled carefully.

The unsettling sound of that jiggling safety value still rattles in my memory. The metal knob would tremble, then break into a wild dance. My mom would run into the kitchen, then screech, "Byeeeee Ruuun. (My dad's name is Byron, but my mom's pressure cooker name for him was always loud and drawn out.) Byeeeeeeee-runnnnn. Come help me get this lid off!"

My fear, every time, was that the pressure of the trapped steam would build to the point that the pot would explode and scald anyone in its vicinity.

Pressure cookers are obviously boiling with energy, but let's look at another, less scarring example. Imagine holding inflated beach balls. You can choose what to do with them, where to put them, where to throw them. They are quite powerless. Not at all dangerous, they are light and easy to handle.

Now imagine being in a pool and holding those beach balls underwater. It requires a tremendous amount of energy to keep them down. It's as if they have a will of their own, and that will is to shoot up out of the water. They were once light and powerless. Now they will fly out of the water with stunning speed, leaving you no control of the direction they move. Pent up energy on display.

We are very much like that pressure cooker and those beach balls when it comes to our emotional world. Energy, no matter what kind, is a powerful force. If it is unaddressed and trapped, it can cause damage to self and others. Here are a few possible signs you might be neglecting your emotional world:

- Lashing out in anger and irritability
- Tightness in your shoulder, neck, or jaw muscles
- Chronic physical pain
- Constant nervousness
- Insomnia
- Big mood swings
- A pattern of being in toxic relationships
- Passive-aggressive behavior
- Over apologizing
- Constant busyness
- Over involved in other people's problems
- Controlling tendencies
- Depression and anxiety
- Serious medical issues (e.g., high blood pressure, chest tightness, digestive problems, migraines)
- Fatigue or low energy
- Changes in appetite

I'm not suggesting a lack of emotional work is always the cause of every symptom and disease on that list. What I am saying is that it is important to be aware of the dangers of emotional suppression.

Whatever emotions you bury, you bury alive. Anything buried alive will do whatever it can to escape.

Beyond that, suppressed emotion results in a suppressed life. Holding in energy can cause damage to you and to others, limiting how you relate and connect, create, and invent. The world needs you and your ideas, your gifts, your talents. Your contributions to your little piece of the world matter. Don't bury them with your emotions.

> ## Whatever emotions you bury, you bury alive.

Emotions Send a Message

I loved my sessions with Timothy. He couldn't come in frequently due to a rigid job schedule, but when he showed up, he always asked thought-provoking questions and was eager to learn. He soaked up every ounce of help I could offer. Timothy was twenty-seven and sober for the first time in his adult life. His parents were both addicted to drugs, essentially leaving him on his own to make his way through life. Not surprisingly, his childhood had been disordered and unpredictable, riddled with abandonment and instability.

To survive the chaos, Timothy started drinking at twelve, using cocaine at fifteen, and addicted to meth by nineteen. His adult life was littered with regret, broken relationships, and bad decisions as the substances did their job to keep his hurt and pain at bay.

Addiction must be understood as an attempt to manage a life that seems unmanageable, a way to find relief. Dr. Gabor Maté, renowned speaker and bestselling author, explores the connection between addiction, stress, and childhood development. He says, "It is impossible to understand addiction without asking what relief the addict finds, or hopes to find, in the drug or the addictive behavior." He says, "Ask not why the addiction, but why the pain."

To say I'm proud of Timothy is an understatement. He's clean from all substances and deeply committed to a life of sobriety. When he first came to counseling, he was clean from cocaine and meth. It took another couple of years and a few more rock bottoms for him to get completely sober.

Sobriety means confronting life head on. It means no more hiding from stress or numbing the hard parts of life. It requires confronting damage done along the way. It also brings one huge obstacle: the emotional world.

Sobriety is embracing the full spectrum of human emotion, from the soaring heights to the depths of despair. Addiction of any type pushes the emotional world aside; the substance sweetly offers a faux joy and an analgesic for the pain. Since he was no longer numbing his emotions, Timothy needed guidance in understanding and regulating them.

He sat on my couch one day, his steel-blue eyes seemed more sad than usual. Refusing to hide from the problem, he went straight at it. "I don't get it. Sometimes I feel down and I watch TV or sleep all day. I'm sober and doing great. Why do I have days like this? I hate it." Timothy had the same idea many people have about emotions: the belief that something bad is happening when challenging emotions show up.

I assured Timothy everything was okay. His body was holding pain, hurt, and regret of all those lost years of addiction, not to mention the neglect he had suffered as a child. Because Timothy started drinking at twelve, we could essentially say his emotional growth was stunted at that age.

Like most people, he assumed emotions simply just go away. I wish it were that simple.

Nothing in the natural world disappears. It only changes form. Our campfire wood doesn't disappear when we burn it; it turns to ash. This is why the list of physical symptoms is important. Our body is our major prophet; it tells the truth. It signals to us about our emotions. If we don't listen, it will speak louder. It will even start screaming. The body can even shut down and send us to the hospital if we don't lean in and pay attention.

Timothy's body was sending him a message. He didn't know how to decipher it. Nothing is wrong with feeling emotional pain or discomfort. Pain is a teaching tool. It is a closet coward; when it is faced, it is no longer scary. Like dear Fred Rogers, the beloved host of Mister Rogers' Neighborhood said, "What is mentionable is manageable."

Our emotions help us define our most courageous and our most heartbreaking times, our strong and weak moments, our fearful and glorious ones. Emotions are not uniquely feminine. Acknowledging them doesn't make a man less masculine. Emotions are a part of our glorious design as humans. They are fuel for life, adding color to all we do.

Like indicator lights on the dashboards of our lives, emotions provide important information, showing what we are excited about, what we enjoy, what makes us uncertain. They help us find our passions, run from danger, fall in love, and slam on the brakes on the freeway. I would not have known I wanted to write this book without the emotions of longing, excitement, and eagerness. The emotions of fear, frustration, and shame all got in the way at times, but were important teachers all the same. Learning to pay attention to and regulate our emotional world is important soul work.

Window of Tolerance

I introduced to Timothy the concept of the Window of Tolerance, a term coined by Dr. Dan Siegel.[6] The Window of Tolerance describes how people manage stressors and function in a way to keep them relationally and emotionally connected. It is the place where people can thrive, practicing both bravery and joy.

The Window of Tolerance is a subjective space, called the optimal zone, characterized by openness, curiosity, flexible thinking, and groundedness. In this space, with full access to your PFC's executive function, you have the ability to regulate your emotions and manage life's stressors. When stress, whether internal or external, expands beyond what is tolerable, the body moves to a different state of the autonomic nervous system, either *hyper*arousal or *hypo*arousal.

Hyperarousal occurs when the sympathetic nervous system—the brain's accelerator—kicks into action. This emotional state is characterized by high energy, emotional outbursts, fear, anxiety, emotional overwhelm, panic, tight muscles, a startled response, irritability.

Hypoarousal occurs when the parasympathetic nervous system—the brain's brake—takes over. In this emotional state, the brain slows down. Key indicators are depression, numbness, emptiness, blank stares, withdrawal, exhaustion, and a flat affect.

---

6   Dan Siegel, a clinical professor of psychiatry at the UCLA School of Medicine and executive director of the Mindsight Institute, developed the metaphor of the Window of Tolerance in 1999.

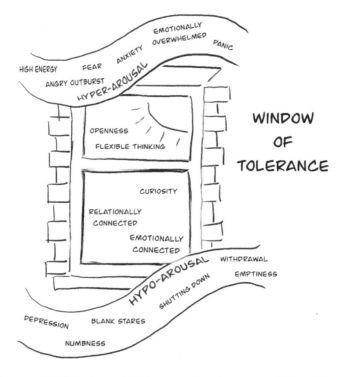

A person's Window of Tolerance is subjective. Each of our windows are unique, shaped by multiple variables, including our personal stories, support systems, biomedical factors, emotional literacy, temperaments, and level of childhood trauma.

Our windows are unique but not fixed. Just as your brain can change and form new habits, you can expand your Window of Tolerance. You can learn to handle a wider range of challenging and difficult emotions.

I started exercising in a new way this past year. The exercise involved more stretching than I had ever done. What was interesting to me was how much my range of motion increased as I worked on small microstretches.

The same thing can happen for our Window of Tolerance. Learning new emotional skills requires that we push our emotional world, but it doesn't have to be extreme. Micro actions enable us to increase our emotional range. Learning how to name, express, and feel a broader range of emotions are small actions that help us grow emotionally. My coach would challenge me to push a muscle group a little bit farther than I thought I could handle. Every time I pushed myself, I noticed I had gotten stronger without even realizing it. The same holds true for the Window of Tolerance. (In the Appendix, you'll find a list of strategies to help you expand your Window of Tolerance.)

Timothy had never made space in his life for sadness or regret. He had never grieved all that he had lost. Brené Brown says it this way: "Owning our stories means reckoning with our feelings and with dark emotions—our fear, anger, aggression, shame, and blame. This isn't easy, but the alternative—denying our stories and disengaging our emotions—means choosing to live our entire lives in the dark."

Timothy's days of sleeping all afternoon were transformed into healthier days, although still hard. He implemented new emotional regulation tools and built a stronger support system. His Window of Tolerance was growing. Feeling sad was still difficult for him, but now he welcomed the challenging emotions, knowing they were necessary for his healing path.

I heard a story once about shark photographers. The interviewer asked the photographer what he did when a shark started swimming toward him. The photographer quickly retorted, "I face him and swim right at 'em."

Face it. That's how we grow our Window of Tolerance. That's how we grow our emotional world. And that's how Timothy learned to live in his newfound sobriety.

Emotional Maintenance

Let's talk about how to face some sharks. Those can be some dangerous, scary creatures! What's the goal for our emotional work, in a nutshell (or maybe a seashell)?

Swim right at it! As easy as that sounds, it can seem counterproductive and hard to do.

Harriet Lerner says it this way, "It is not fear that stops you from doing the brave and true thing in your daily life; rather, the problem is avoidance. You want to feel comfortable, so you avoid doing or saying the thing that evokes fear and other difficult emotions. Avoidance will make you feel less vulnerable in the short run, but it will never make you less afraid." In other words, what we resist, persists.

In 2016, Chris and I bought our vintage teardrop camper from a man in Galveston. He purchased it from the man who designed and custom-built it, but evidently neither of them spent much time camping in it. Both of our dads immediately suggested we buy new tires. They said the existing tires were likely dry rotted since the camper had been stored outside. We had a quick turnaround time from the date of purchase to when we were leaving on our maiden voyage: a ten-day, 3,000-mile camping trip to the canyons out west. We brought it home, painted beautiful turquoise and white stripes down the side of the shiny aluminum exterior and left two weeks later.

Oh, I forgot to say, we didn't listen to our dads.

You guessed it. They were right. Only nine short hours after pulling out of our driveway, a tire blew out on I-40 on the outskirts of Tucumcari, New Mexico. One hour of maintenance—simply driving to the tire store—would have saved six hours on the trip. We had to change the flat off a busy freeway, drive an hour on one of those hilariously small spare tires, and wait for two new tires to be installed. Additionally, we now had a damaged vintage striped teardrop with dings and dents from where the tire shrapnel flung chunks of rubber and steel onto our freshly painted stripes.

Soul adventurers, emotional maintenance is as valuable as tire maintenance.

Research in the social sciences confirms the value of understanding the emotional world. High EQ (emotional quotient) is essential to thriving in homes and workplaces. Daniel Goldman, in his primers on emotional intelligence, says, "for jobs of all kinds at all levels, on average, emotional intelligence was twice as important as cognitive ability in terms of distinguishing competencies."

Did you get that? How we understand our emotions is *twice* as important as how smart we are.

I want to keep from calling emotions good or bad, easy or hard. For our purposes, I will use the terms positive and challenging. Positive emotions create affirmative or calming energy; challenging emotions create discomfort regardless of their intensity.

There is not a human among us who grew up with both parents fully emotionally present in each and every moment, coaching in a healthy way through all ups and downs of life's experiences. We are raised by imperfect people who leave imperfect imprints on us. Few of us grew up understanding the full range of what we felt. One of the greatest losses most of us experience is the ability to name, feel, and process our emotions. Most of us don't even realize we have lost this. Emotions need to be seen, to be validated, to be soothed. The way to live a brave and joyful life is to see and validate your own emotional world. You can't give others what you have not first given yourself.

> The way to live a brave and joyful life is to see and validate your own emotional world. You can't give others what you have not first given yourself.

We have uniqueness about us, making our emotional world as distinct as our fingerprints. Our emotions show up differently and are experienced differently. That said, there are some general strategies we all need to implement to help us along the path. I'm giving you my most tried and tested tools I give my clients.

It's time to get practical. I tell my clients I love to be practical, but practical does not mean it's fairy dust! Learning how to understand and regulate emotions takes practice.

We'll start our practice with four key words that make it safe to explore your emotional world: slow and soft, curious and kind.

Slow and Soft

Nothing is more frustrating for me than being told to *calm down* when I'm upset. Yes, yes, I know I should calm down! For some nonsensical reason, it makes me feel angrier. Being *told* to do it seems to make it harder.

I have a new option for us: slow and soft. It is more helpful to put this strategy into practice than telling myself (or others) to calm down.

Slow, deep, cleansing breaths, movement, stretching, and grounding strategies will help you be gentle with yourself. It will help you stay regulated and bring you into your Window of Tolerance. Soft begets soft, which keeps the PFC online and helps you face those challenging emotions.. The back brain is fast; the front brain is slow. You are in no hurry. There is no problem to be solved, only an emotion to process. This allows you to stay open and relational with God, self, and others. An emotion is like a wave, not lasting more than a few minutes if you ride it slowly and softly.

Curious and Kind

To stay in the PFC, it is vital to stay out of judgment and criticism. Curiosity and kindness are front brain processes. The back brain wants to find the enemy, to move toward blame, quick decisions, hasty actions, or withdrawal. Stay connected to what your body is feeling and stay open. Validate your emotions by saying to yourself, *Of course I'm feeling sad. It is okay to feel sadness.* This soothes and offers acceptance of self. To stay in the PFC, remind yourself of the relationships you want to be connected to and remind yourself that feeling your emotions is a part of being whole and complete. My three favorite phrases when exploring the emotional world are as follows:

It's interesting.

Of course I feel . . .

I'm noticing . . .

Those are words of acceptance. They are kind words. It does not help to tell emotions to go away or to get mad at their appearance. Does a red light turn green faster by yelling at it? I've tried. Many, many times. Does getting frustrated with a flight delay help the plane take off quicker? I wish. Our emotions can seem irritating and frustrating. They need to be treated with kindness.

Look at the circle. The circle represents an emotion you are feeling. Let's say it is sadness. Your body is built to process your emotion. Emotions are not permanent. They are energy moving through your body. As you breathe and use the strategies of slow and soft, curious and kind, the emotion will process through your body. If you get frustrated *at the sadness* (or afraid, mad, weary of it), you have now created a jagged ring around it, making it larger. This is now like a saw blade moving through your nervous system, ripping it up, activating your stress response system, moving you out of your Window of Tolerance. The frustration *at the sadness* is the problem, not the sadness itself. It is now more difficult to process this emotion, which leads you to believe you cannot do it. Next time you feel sadness, the body remembers the saw blade and says, *Umm, heck no. Not doing it. That emotion is too much for me to handle!* See how that works? Use the acceptance phrases above. They will help you make sense of the emotion and care well for yourself while you feel it.

Name It and Tame It

You'll hear the story about my Spanish-speaking skills a little later, but here is a preview: It was difficult to travel through Spain as a sub-par Spanish speaker. It is also difficult to manage emotions without a robust emotional vocabulary. You need to know emotional language!

Naming what you feel and accepting your emotions is how you regulate them: Name it and tame it! When emotion hits, it is helpful to expand the emotional vocabulary so you can practice naming what you feel with more specificity. Check in with your emotional experience and find words to describe what you're feeling. This practice will help with self-regulation. It might sound like, *"I am feeling my heart race, and my thoughts are spinning. This feels like anxiety. I am also feeling some sadness. Both of those emotions are okay for me to feel."*

> Find a list of emotional words and spend time looking over it on a regular basis. The downloadable feeling chart on my website is a good place to start! ChristineWolfHoover.com.

We did it! We have our emotional world packed and ready. We have one more essential piece of equipment to get into our suitcases. You might need to move some things around because we will be packing some hula hoops, and they tend to take up a little more than their fair share of space.

Do the Work

When reflecting on your Window of Tolerance, do you tend to move toward *hyper*arousal or *hypo*arousal? What are the specific ways you react when hooked by big emotion? Name one new strategy you can practice this week to regulate your emotions in a healthier way.

Do the Joy

Go outside and notice five things you love. Notice the unique characteristics of each. Spend ten minutes breathing and relaxing.

YOUR BOUNDARIES

"No" is a complete sentence.

—— ANNE LAMOTT ——

I f you've never stayed in a yurt, you should give it a try! We stayed the night in a custom-built yurt when we were in Nova Scotia while camping our way around Cape Breton Island. It was our one *special* excursion; every other night was spent sleeping in the camper-van. Nestled on the banks of a tranquil river, the colorful, whimsical yurt was an unforgettable experience. We had a charming campfire and a dark, starry night. The evening was dreamy.

The next morning as we loaded the van, I was scheming a way to stay longer on our trip and come back to the yurt for another night. Remember, I'm the *If you Give a Mouse A Cookie* travel girl! Chris looked firmly at me and said, "No, honey. We're sticking with our itinerary."

I hated his answer, but I knew he was right. Boundaries are a part of life. We all must know how to accept and respect them. I'm a slow learner on this one.

Samantha started sessions with me, honestly admitting her resentment toward her husband, Brandon, who was unwilling to come to counseling. Married for sixteen years, they had two elementary-aged children. Samantha was utterly exhausted from working full time and carrying the lion's share of the household chores. After work, she drove the kids to soccer practices and dance lessons. She dragged in the door at 6:30 but managed to rally the energy to start dinner and wash a few loads of clothes. Brandon worked full time as well but spent his evenings unwinding in the living room, watching YouTube, or fiddling with projects in the garage.

Samantha didn't like to think of herself as an angry person, but she couldn't deny the reality. Fury oozed out of her the moment she walked in the door. She nagged Brandon to help. She slammed doors. She sighed at him whenever he walked by. When he did help, she would glare at him, silently obsessing over the litany of things he *wasn't* getting done. She nagged and begged some more. Nothing changed.

Vacillating between resentment and hopelessness, she felt stuck. From her perspective, her challenging emotions were Brandon's fault. She constantly attempted to get him to help with household responsibilities or interact with the family. She desperately wanted to live a more peaceful life. All she could see was his failure to live up to her expectations. To be fair, there was much to see. What she couldn't see was the part she played in this chaotic dance.

Samantha was justified in her frustration with Brandon's behavior but mistaken in feeling powerless to change the dynamic. Samantha desperately needed tools to manage herself in new ways.

She needed boundaries. So do you. And clearly, so do I.

Your boundaries are the final piece of gear essential for your soul adventure.

For your soul to be healthy, to live a life of bravery and joy, you need to know what is yours to control *and* what is not yours to control. Establishing boundaries is about learning to live with healthy limits, grounded and centered. If you don't learn how to practice using your voice and creating healthy boundaries, you'll end up feeling the way

Samantha did when she walked into my office: burned out, resentful, and exhausted.

I have a hunch that's not what you want for your life. Samantha sure didn't.

Samantha was not able to set and hold a boundary with Brandon, and as a result, she was morphing into a person she didn't even like. Let me say this: Brandon *was* in the wrong for many of the issues they faced. But since he was unwilling to come to sessions, Samantha had to learn heathier habits for herself. She knew she needed to learn how to be less emotionally reactive and more firm about his lack of participation in their marriage.

Pack Your Hula Hoop

Samantha desperately needed to get in her hula hoop. Why a hula hoop, you might ask? Hula hoops are my go-to metaphor for teaching personal boundaries. You may think a hula hoop is too big to fit in your suitcase, but you need to do whatever it takes to cram that sucker in.

Let me explain. Wherever you are right now, imagine a hula hoop on the floor. Picture yourself standing in the middle of it, every part of you encircled by the hoop. The hula hoop defines your boundaries. It shows you where you begin and someone else ends. Everything inside the hula hoop is your responsibility. Inside your hula hoop are *your*...

- emotions
- thoughts
- actions
- values and integrity
- attitudes
- behaviors
- likes and dislikes
- beliefs
- choices and preference

Your hula hoop shows you what is yours and what isn't yours. The boundaries you set also require you to define your wants and needs and take responsibility for the life you are living. Not the life you wish you had. Not the one you thought you were going to have. The life directly in front of you.

Boundaries are not selfish, nor are they walls that keep you isolated. They are connection-creating rather than connection-hindering tools, which makes them vital to healthy relationships. Boundaries can be physical, emotional, interpersonal, or intrapersonal; they are about safety. The purpose of boundaries is to create a protective barrier that allows you to develop your voice, remain true to your values, and maintain a sense of peace.

Boundary work requires you to stop looking *out there* for the solutions to your problems. When you know what's yours to control and keep your focus there, you can move forward in a healthy way when trouble arises.

My dad was a beef cattle rancher, which means I heard him talk a lot about fences. As in "That dumb bull tried to jump the fence again and messed up the fence line." Or "Last night someone ran off the road and knocked the fence down. Hop in the truck, we need to go fix it." Fence lines are a non-negotiable necessity for ranch life. My dad's cattle needed to stay on his property safely where they belonged. The neighbors' animals needed to do the same. Seems like we were always mending fences, and it was hard work!

The truth is, fixing fences is a lot like setting and maintaining your boundaries. It isn't all that easy.

Samantha didn't know how to talk to Brandon and express her need for a more equitable partnership around the house and the lack of connection in their marriage. She was afraid of upsetting him. The stress of doing everything for her family pushed her outside her Window of Tolerance, moving her into the hyperarousal state. She over-functioned, allowing the anxiety to move her to do what Brandon should have been doing for himself. Brandon under-functioned. His anxiety caused him to shut down. He pulled away and avoided.

The more she over-functioned, the more he under-functioned. Down and down they went, in a spiral of disconnection and frustration. Samantha spent most of her time looking inside of Brandon's hula hoop, describing what he didn't do, trying to figure out why he did what he did. She obsessed over his failures and the way he wasn't showing up in their marriage. She wanted to figure *him* out.

All she wanted to talk about in our sessions was Brandon and why he acted the way he did. I would gently redirect back to her hula hoop by asking, "Is his behavior in your hula hoop or his? Is the reason behind his actions in his hula hoop or yours?"

From the Beginning

It is much easier to describe someone else's flaws and bad behaviors than to take responsibility for your own flaws and bad behaviors. It's easier but unhelpful. It is not our job to analyze and figure other people out. Not only is it not our job, but it is also not possible to fully understand the heart of another person.

It's been this way since the beginning. When we return to the Genesis narrative, it is almost comical to see the rapid-fire finger-pointing.

> "Who told you that you were naked?" the Lord God asked. "Have you eaten from the tree whose fruit I commanded you not to eat?"
>
> The man replied, "It was the woman you gave me who gave me the fruit, and I ate it."
>
> Then the Lord God asked the woman, "What have you done?"
>
> "The serpent deceived me," she replied. "That's why I ate it."
>
> —Genesis 3:8–13, NLT

The lack of personal responsibility here is astounding. God asks clarifying questions, attempting to bring Adam and Eve to a place of truth and repentance. A place of reconnection. But when God asks them about what they have done, in their shame, they hide, deny, and shift the blame, convinced that someone else caused their sinful actions.

Humans haven't changed much. We're still great at focusing on everyone else's flaws and forgetting that we play a role in every relationship.

Defining Your Vulnerable Self

"Samantha," I said firmly. "When I ask how *you* are feeling, you tell me more about *him*. When I ask what *you* want to do differently, you tell me what *he* is doing or not doing. Describe yourself. What's going on inside your hula hoop? What are you feeling right now?"

I gently placed my hand over my heart. I asked her to do the same. "Samantha, I want to know about what is happening *inside* of you." I looked directly at her hand and nodded my head, giving her hand the permission it needed to help connect her to what was secretly tucked away in her soul.

Like all our work on our soul adventure, it is vitally important to reconnect our bodies to our experiences. God built us with a natural system of distress, meaning our bodies and our lives begin to feel distress when we are living in unhealthy patterns. It is imperative that we listen to that distress.

Samantha's exhaustion was a message. Her resentment was a message. She needed to honor the story her body was telling. I wanted Samantha to allow her hand to bring a nurturing and gentle touch to her heart, giving herself permission to name what she was feeling and what she needed. All this time she thought she needed Brandon to do more; *he* was the problem. Now it was time for her to lean in to hear what her body was truly attempting to tell her.

She listened. Samantha was tired of the dance. Actually, she was exhausted by it. She knew she needed to learn how to be vulnerable and express what she needed. When she talked about Brandon, she was fast and clear, able to describe his behavior in meticulous detail. As I invited her to describe herself, the words took time to form. Thick tears welled up in her tender eyes. "I am so sad," she said quietly. "I feel let down. Stuck. I'm ashamed because this was the exact way my mom treated my dad, and I always sort of felt sorry for him. He could never do anything right. She was always so mad at him. I don't want to be like that."

Underneath that tough exterior was someone who was sad, not mad.

Now we were getting somewhere. Samantha was practicing the important skills of listening to her body, leaning into her own painful emotions, and owning what was in her hula hoop. She was beginning to understand she needed to talk about herself instead of focusing solely on Brandon. She was learning to name her emotions, family story, values, behaviors, responses, limits, and desires. If she wanted to hold to her value of not yelling like her mom did, she needed to learn how to make that value actionable by drawing boundaries—and holding to them.

People tell me all the time, "I drew a boundary, but it didn't work."

My response is always the same: "Then it wasn't a boundary. Boundaries always work." A boundary always works because a boundary describes what *I* will do. You know what doesn't work? Telling someone else what to do. We can't make anyone do anything. You can't even make a two-year-old eat a pea. A few basic boundary statements include:

- I'm not okay with that.
- I don't have an answer right now. I will get back to you.
- No, that will not work for my schedule.
- I'm sorry this is a hard time for you, but I am not able to support you financially.

Let's look at two people, Bella and Ann, working in an office together. Bella frequently comes in late because she stays up late playing video games and watching TV, then sleeps through her alarm. Ann answers the phones in Bella's absence (which is Bella's primary job) and neglects her morning responsibilities. The pressure of doing both their jobs is stressful, and Ann has mentioned it, but Bella blew her off.

After more than six months of stress-filled mornings, Ann decides to draw a boundary. "You need to stop coming in late and making me cover for you," she says.

Now, can she *make* Bella come in on time? She cannot. Which means that her statement, as heartfelt as it was, is not a boundary. Bella's disregard for time is beyond her control. It's no surprise that Bella blows off Ann again.

Finally, Ann realizes she only has control over what she will *do* differently when Bella is late. Her behavior (not her wishes) is what creates the boundary.

Crabs in a Bucket

In the early days of Alcoholics Anonymous, those who studied the family systems of alcoholics noticed an interesting pattern. An alcoholic almost always exists in a system in which another person enables the bad behavior. The alcoholic is addicted to the substance, and the enabler is addicted to fixing the alcoholic or to staying angry at the alcoholic. These are not conscious choices, but patterned ways of behaving. Neither person knows how to take responsibility for self in a way that brings meaningful change, so both feel trapped managing something unmanageable.

The scenario has been likened to two crabs stuck in a bucket. Just as one crab is grasping for the edge of the bucket to escape, the other crab grabs the escapee's dangling leg, pulling them back down into the bucket. Round and round they go. Both stuck. Both miserable. Both trying to get free, yet both thwarting the other's futile attempts at escape. It would be comical if it weren't so sad.

So how do you get out of the bucket?

First, you have to *want* to get out of the bucket.

You've heard the adage, "better the devil you know than the devil you don't." Sometimes being stuck seems better, safer, or more comfortable than whatever is beyond the walls of our buckets. Bucket living feels easier, even if it isn't working.

I've been stuck in buckets of my own. When I opened my private practice, I couldn't crawl out of the bucket of undervaluing my professional worth. I believed that a nice Christian woman who runs her own business should offer her services for cut-rate prices. It felt greedy to charge no-show fees for chronic absenteeism.

In my personal life, I couldn't crawl out of the bucket of saying yes to every ask: every invitation, every multi-level marketing party, every volunteer need. I believed that I didn't have the right to set a limit on others' demands on my time. I know I'm not alone in this. I've talked with clients who feel the implicit pressure to say yes. In our three decades of church ministry, I've noticed that there's an expectation that women are to be experienced as kind, nice, and always willing to say yes to meeting others' needs. Typically, no one specifically *teaches* that it is selfish to say no, but it is common for women to condemn themselves as such when they deny a request.

How do I know? They tell me in counseling sessions. Month after month, year after year, they tell me they are weary and worn out. They feel selfish if they honestly say what they feel and what they need.

In the short run, it may seem easier to keep saying yes, but that also means staying weary and resentful toward the person who pulls you back down in the bucket.

It can feel scary to navigate life any other way. Change *is* hard. Many of us, me included, were not given the tools we needed to know how to have a healthy, assertive voice. Some of us never saw clear modeling of hula hoops. Climbing out of those buckets requires that we learn new boundary language and strategies to show up as healthier versions of ourselves.

Practice Getting Out of the Bucket

Remember when I backpacked through Europe? The first leg of the trip was the four-week Spanish immersion class I needed to complete my final hours of Spanish all in one swoop and finish my degree.

Please don't miss that word, *immersion*. The Spanish teachers did *not* teach Spanish using English. They only taught Spanish *in* Spanish. Of course they did! They were Spanish professors at a Spanish university.

Somehow, I hadn't considered this when I excitedly signed up. All my brain heard was, "Eight hours of credit in four weeks."

I had barely squeaked my way through my first two Spanish classes at Texas A&M. My college bestie and roomie, Karla, quizzed me for hours on Spanish vocabulary using my handwritten notecards. To this day, she can tell you with stunning accuracy how below average I was as a Spanish speaker. She claims our test prep nights are one of her college core memories. I was famous for combining silly Spanish and English phrases, saying things like, "I have a *cabeza* ache" (headache), holy *vaca* (holy cow), "*Me gusto* you very much" (I love you very much.) My silly antics were the perfect ruse to hide my sparse Spanish-speaking skills.

Back to Spain. I was forced to conjugate those crazy Spanish vocab words in real time, in front of real people. I could barely conjugate words in slow motion, like on paper for a test, but to be conversational, as in wake up and talk to my host home family about how I slept and what I wanted for breakfast? *Are you kidding me?* I did lots and lots of head-nodding and smiling, that's for sure. My language skills were lacking.

Back to Samantha. She also needed to practice a new language: the language of boundaries. She wanted to get out of her bucket. For her healing, Samantha was going to need to dig down to find her vulnerable emotions and draw healthy boundaries to heal from her cycle of resentment and exhaustion.

She learned how to define herself and ask for what she needed with actionable consequences. She understood the need to hold Brandon responsible for his own irresponsibility. In his book *Boundaries*, Henry Cloud says, "To rescue people from the natural consequences of their behavior is to render them powerless." Her nagging was leaving them both powerless.

Together, we practiced new ways for Samantha to express herself. I would pretend to be Brandon, giving all the excuses in the world, as I imagined he would. (I absolutely *love* doing this exercise in session, getting the chance to put on my thespian hat. Hey, I had a leading role in One Act play in high school, and we won district. I have some skills! When I implement this strategy, I overplay all the emotions and conversation. The exaggeration actually mimics how stressful it can feel to have these kinds of conversations.)

Something important to note here is that this roleplaying put Samantha's habit-forming brain into action. As we practiced, her brain created new pathways for this novel way of thinking and feeling and acting. The more we practiced, the more we laid down a path in the wheat field. Additionally, my big, exaggerated emotions activated her stress responses system. I was keeping her social engagement system online, in the PFC, while she learned to use her assertive voice. Practice makes patterns, and with our roleplaying, she was creating positive patterns.

One of Samantha's fears in leaning into her own boundary work was her fear of divorce. She was afraid of her children being from a broken home. I gently assured her the only hope for their marriage was for her to show up with honesty and integrity. Their daughters were already being affected by his avoidance and her resentment. Facing the damage she and Brandon were doing to each other was the only way out of the bucket.

She learned how to use vulnerable "I" language and stay away from the criticism of "you always" statements. She learned how to show empathy for Brandon without rescuing him from the consequences of his behavior. After much practice and hard work, she let Brandon know she wanted a healthier relationship, and she needed him to show up in more tangible, meaningful ways if their marriage was going to make it. She was clear and specific, naming exactly what she needed and how she would respond, all the while staying in her values to be kind and firm, gracious and honest.

In her calm, confident state, Samantha was also able to see that it was just as hard for Brandon to engage emotionally as it was for her to show up with a gentle, assertive voice.

Are you dying to know how it's going for them? I'll fill you in after we talk about an energy crisis in our midst.

The Emotional Work of Boundaries

Our soul adventure requires energy! When we run low on emotional energy, all types of unpleasant things can happen. We wonder why we often feel exhausted, irritable, and short-tempered. Most people assume their problem lies in time management. I beg to differ. The problem is not time management, but energy management. It is not time conservation, but energy conservation. I've mentioned numerous times about a lack of boundaries producing both resentment and exhaustion. Let me show you how this works:

> Lack of boundaries = drained energy
> Drained energy = exhaustion and resentment
> Exhaustion and resentment = irritability, frustration,
> anger outbursts

Let's start by talking about money. Imagine I walk up to you in the morning, handing you $100 in $1 bills. I tell you, "Good morning, dear friend! This money is all yours. Spend it making your day what you want it to be. Enjoy every single bit of it!"

Then, seconds later, I flip the script. "Instead of spending it on what you need, throw it out of the car window or in the trash, $1 at a time, all day long, until you have nothing left. Once you throw it out, you are not able to get it back." I have a sneaking suspicion you would argue with me about having to throw it away. What if I did this day after day after day? Wouldn't you want to hold to that money so *you* can spend it?

Let's use the money as a metaphor for emotional energy.

Emotional energy is like cash. It is ours to spend on living our life. We are given a mysterious, invisible, yet sufficient resource of energy to manage our days, our lives, our relationships, careers, and hobbies. The energy is accumulated through rest, nutrition, exercise, meaningful spiritual practices, life-giving relationships, healthy life/work balance, and so on.

If energy is like cash, why throw away what you need?

Hula hoops show us what is ours and what is not ours. We throw away energy when we attempt to fix a problem that is not ours or rescue someone from the natural consequences of their own behavior.

These three Cs say it succinctly: We cannot *change*, *cure*, or *control* other people. Let me illustrate how we spend our energy (emotional currency) trying to change, control, or cure other people.

I've been drawing these basic stick figures in session for years, which clearly demonstrates my limited artistic abilities.

Take a look at the drawing. It adds a new layer to the hula hoops

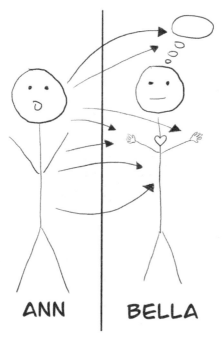

principles. The line divides Ann and Bella. The line represents a natural law God established: the Law of Responsibility. This law illuminates the reality that we are only able to control what is on our side of the line, which includes all the same items as what is in our hula hoop: our thoughts, emotions, behaviors, attitudes, preferences, etc.

The line is not a wall. It is a natural boundary, showing what we can control and what we can't control. On my side of the line is ME. My thoughts, behaviors, attitudes, beliefs, values, preferences. The other side of the line is the person with whom I am in relationship.

Now let's look at the arrows. In this scenario, let's go back to the two coworkers, Ann and Bella.

Ann is frustrated because Bella keeps coming in late. Ann knows she cannot control anything on Bella's side of the line, so Ann is working on the boundary of not answering the phone for Bella. The drawings represent three of the primary things for which each is responsible: thoughts, emotions, and behaviors.

Ann is considering saying something to Bella, but her fear of having a healthy boundary is creating a loop of overthinking. Here are her thoughts:

I don't want Bella to be mad at me.

I feel bad she is so tired. I don't want her to be rude to customers.

I don't want to hurt Bella's feelings.

I don't want Bella to think I'm stuck up now.

I don't want Bella to think I don't care about her. I shouldn't be so selfish.

I don't want Bella to get in trouble with our boss because of me.

I don't want Bella to think I'm trying to get her fired.

Every one of her thoughts is represented by an arrow crossing over the line. Remember, she has no control over Bella's thoughts, feelings, or actions.

Let's pretend Ann gets $100 a day of that emotional currency we were talking about. If those thoughts and worries cost her $5 each, how long would it take her to run out of energy? If she cycles through these thoughts like these four times a day, she's going to be over budget and out of energy.

Math time.

7 arrows x $5 emotional currency: $35

$35	$100
x 4	−$140
$140	−40 (If this book were in color, that number would be red.)

Ann spends $140 of her day's allowance of energy thinking about something she cannot control. She is now in the negative. Bella is only one person in Ann's life. How many other people are in Ann's life where she might be throwing away more of her emotional energy? Instead of contemplating how to use her boundary language, assert her needs, and have actionable consequences, she is left drained of her emotional capacities.

Math never lies, right? Exhaustion and resentment are the natural consequence of not living within healthy limits. Ann was spending all her energy thinking about Bella's hula hoop instead of focusing on how she could be honest about what she needed and allowing the natural consequences of Bella's behavior to stay in *Bella's* hula hoop, where it belonged.

Hula Hoop Heroes

I am so excited to fill you in on Samantha. Watching her grow and change has been an absolute joy and honor. She was exhausted by being stuck in the bucket, tired of the cycle. The nagging and over-functioning were not working anyway.

Vulnerability was her only way forward. After two months of working and practicing with me, she knew it was time to draw a firm, clear boundary.

She quit the nagging about household chores, waiting to see how he responded. Not much had changed. He continued to be disengaged. This was it. She was ready. She asked to meet him for coffee one morning after she got the girls off to school. Just like she had practiced, she shared her feelings and made her boundaries clear. Without yelling, she calmly said, "I'm no longer going to get on to you about your emotional absence in our home. I know I drive you crazy with my endless nagging. If you choose to ignore us in the evenings and not participate in the family activities, you can find another place to live where you can scroll all you want. I value a healthy emotional environment for me and the kids, and I invite you to join me in that. I am sad and hurt that we are so disconnected. I have felt abandoned in our marriage and in running the household alone. I would love for us to be partners in life, but I know what we are doing is not working. I love you, and I hope you choose us." She left it at that. No begging. No nagging. The ball was in his court. To be more accurate, the choice was in his hula hoop. Where it belonged.

You know what he chose? He chose his family. It wasn't quick or easy. He moved out to live with his parents, started attending a men's group at their church, and eventually went to counseling on his own to learn how to handle stress and be emotionally connected. It was hard for all of them for another year or so. She leaned into her faith during these months, seeking wisdom from God and support from friends.

In the end, they made it. And all of that can be traced back to Samantha listening to her own body's messages, understanding her hula hoops, and asserting her actionable wants and needs in a vulnerable way.

Let's pan the camera over to Ann and Bella's office. Time to check in with what Ann and Sleepy-Bella have been up to.

Bella continued dragging in late. Ann realized she could not continue to give the situation all the energy she had been giving it. She was ready to use "I" statements, making them actionable. Bella came in late again. Ann asked if she could talk to Bella after lunch. She went to her desk, sat down, and said, "Hey, I know it's really hard for you to get here on time. I understand you are not a morning person. But I'm not going to cover for you when you are late. It's not my job. If this continues, I will follow company policy and talk to our supervisor about what I should do when you aren't here to answer the phone."

Is that uncomfortable? Absolutely it is. It might even feel rude. But if Ann continued answering the phone, she would become more stressed and resentful, which is a far worse problem over the long haul than a few moments of discomfort. She was terrified of having to talk to her supervisor, but as it turns out, Bella heard her *loud* and *clear*. Once Bella knew Ann was serious, she took responsibility for her tardiness and made a concerted effort to get to work on time.

We often hear the dramatic, sad stories of people never changing, relationships souring, coworkers giving each other the stink eye from across the cubicles. It doesn't have to be that way. Our souls are meant to change and grow, to embrace new learnings and shift perspectives. This happens primarily through challenging situations in our lives.[7]

Hula hoop heroes bring us all hope. They are proof of the power of knowing what is ours and what is not ours.

Let's start a revolution of practicing healthy boundaries so we can live brave and joy-filled lives. All I can hear in my mind is the band Foreigner, belting out some edited lyrics, "Hula. Hoop. Heroes. Got stars in their eyes."

Believe it or not, we're done packing! Whew! You now have all the essential gear for our adventure. I hope you can see by now that packing for the journey is part of the journey itself. The preparations you've made have already moved you toward living a braver, more adventurous, and beautiful life.

In the next section, you'll find travel advisories. A few challenges wait around the bend, things that can wreak havoc on your soul adventure if you're not prepared. Seasoned travelers, particularly those who travel to foreign lands, know to check the travel advisory for their destinations. Some advice includes health precautions, such as vaccinations for diseases you've never had to worry about before. To prepare for my trip to Uganda in 2013, I had to get a vaccine for both yellow fever and typhoid, and I also carried a prescription for a malaria medicine. Some warnings seem minor, such as watch out for pickpockets. If you've ever had your passport or wallet stolen (or simply lost it) while traveling abroad, you know that it isn't a minor inconvenience. Other warnings are more serious, urging travelers to reconsider their destination or abandon the trip altogether. Soul adventuring will take you places you've longed and feared to go. With your essential gear, you're equipped to handle the journey. My job as your sacred guide and co-traveler is to make sure you know what to watch out for.

More adventure is ahead!

---

7 Firm boundaries can potentially intensify an abusive relationship. If you are unsafe, seek safety immediately. Find support and contact your local domestic abuse crisis center or the National Abuse Hotline at 1-800-799-7233.

Do the Work

Is there a situation where you are allowing your boundaries to be crossed right now? What is one step you can take to set a healthy limit for yourself?

Do the Joy

Take a walk while listening to a song that makes you feel energized and happy.

PART 3

TRAVEL ADVISORIES

Caution:
Hitchhikers, Ruts, and
Roadblocks Ahead

− 8 −

THE UNWANTED PASSENGER

Whatever we cannot name reveals the
insidious bondage we still exist in.

— RICH VILLODAS —

Final nights on long camping trips are about clean-up. Repacking bags, warming leftovers, throwing away trash. We roll up charging cords, dig between seats, hang up wet towels.

It was our last night of camping New Zealand's north island; the clean-up routine was in full swing. The young couple in the campsite next to ours was clearly doing the same thing. Camping culture is friendly. I love the sense of comradery. *Where are you headed next? Where did you hike? How long are you traveling?* Travelers feel a sense of shared community, as if we are all in this together.

The sites at this campground were close to each other. We noticed the couple seemed bothered by something. They aggressively shook out their food and blankets. She looked particularly frantic, dumping cracker boxes and chip bags upside down. They weren't casually cleaning out their stuff. It was obvious they were looking for something.

As I walked around our van, I heard her gasping, now violently shaking the Triscuit box. I made eye contact with her, gently asking, "Hey, is everything okay?"

In a sweet English accent, she gasped, "NO! It's horrid! We wondered all week if there was something in our van. We've heard something rustling and chewing during the night. We saw the mouse this morning! On our bed! All our food has nibble holes in them! It's revolting. Simply revolting."

An unwanted passenger on their adventure.

No one wants an unwanted traveler to tag along, but I have some bad news for you. Like our young English couple, we, too, have an unwanted passenger on our soul adventure.

Chances are good that you encounter this unwanted passenger more frequently than you realize. That's certainly been true in my life. It took me years to identify and face down this unwanted passenger that wreaked havoc on my soul as I wrote this book. I almost waved the white flag and surrendered my dream to this unseen enemy. But I'll tell you something: Facing this unwelcome force has been the most healing adventure of my adult life.

So, who or what is this malevolent, unwanted passenger?

Call It by Its Name

Professor Dumbledore wisely told Harry Potter, "Call him Voldemort, Harry. Always use the proper name for things. Fear of a name increases fear of the thing itself."

What is the name of our unwanted passenger?

Shame.

Shame is a key element in understanding relational distress, the damage of trauma, the addictive cycle, and the destructive emotional storms we all experience. Most of the work I do revolves around the impact of shame on the lives of my clients.

We need to call shame by name to face it. Right about now, you might feel tempted to check out or skip to the next chapter, convinced that shame is something *other* people struggle with, but not you. Perhaps you see the word shame and shrug it off.

I really don't ever feel shame.

I had a great childhood and a good life. Shame never really comes up for me.

Shame is not a problem for me. I don't struggle with that.

I've worked through all my shame in the past.

I don't get embarrassed easily. Things don't bother me.

Taking big risks is easy for me. I don't struggle with feeling confident in what I can do.

I've heard all those arguments before. I've said many of them myself. But hear me on this: Shame is present, in some form or fashion, in all our lives. I am a confident person, *and* I still struggle with shame at times. I help people through shame, yet shame shows up for me. You can be strong and feel shame, be competent and feel shame. You can be a healthy person, and shame can still be at work in the background.

We struggle with shame because we are human.

Shame can skulk around for years before being discovered. As I said, you might have been battling with this unwanted passenger for years without knowing what you were fighting. Ignoring or denying its existence gives it even more power to do more damage. Naming shame as the enemy, on the other hand, gives you an advantage in this battle.

I wish we could just uninvite shame from our journey. That, unfortunately, is impossible. Shame will be with us. We can't kick the hitchhiker out of the car. Our best hope is to acknowledge its presence, banish it to the backseat of our psyches, learn to build resilience strategies, and limit the harm it does along the way.

Nothing motivates me to type these words more than the hope that you will face this force with fury and minimize any further damage it intends to bring into your life.

The shame I experienced during my writing journey dug deeply into my personhood, leading me into creativity-robbing perfectionism and soul-destroying comparison. Shame was stealing my confidence, numbing my delight, and hampering my hope. How could I reclaim what was mine and do the thing God called me to do?

Write about it.

So you could read about it.

Just as shame attempted to stop me, shame will stop at *nothing* to stop you. This unwanted passenger is on a mission from the enemy to keep us from living our fullest and deepest lives. Our souls are meant to be at rest and at peace, to be brave and filled with deep, relational joy. Shame disorients us, keeping us lost and afraid. And alone.

Together, we can build shame-resilience and live braver, more joy-filled lives. We will do exactly as the campers Chris and I met in New Zealand did. We will leave no corner uninspected, look in every nook and cranny, seal off every possible entry way to stop it from sneaking in and causing any further damage.

What Is Shame?

Researcher Brené Brown defines shame this way: "The intensely painful feeling or experience of believing that we are flawed and therefore unworthy of love and belonging. We feel like something we've experienced, done, or failed to do makes us unworthy of connection." She goes on to say, "Shame often leaves us feeling immobilized, or worse, feeling ready to strike out as a way of offloading the pain of disconnection."

When shame takes hold, it triggers a cascade of intense emotions, self-critical thoughts, and bodily dysregulation. This is why we prepared for this journey by packing our integrated brain, our stories, our emotional world, and our boundaries. To render the unwanted passenger powerless, we will need all our essential gear.

Shame affects every human. We can't abolish it, but we can and must learn to identify and understand it. Curt Thompson has written extensively on the intersection of neuroscience and theology of shame. He describes how evil uses shame:

The voice of evil has a very different intention than God does. Its intention is to twist and sully the story of joy and creativity that God is working so hard to tell. And I suggest that evil's maleficent intent is wielded no more forcefully (yet subtly as part of its tactical prowess) than through the use of shame.

Shame is not a neutral player on the field. It is the emotional feature out of which all that we call sin emerges. As such, in the biblical narrative when we experience shame, we are not simply encountering one of an array of possible emotions; rather we are engaging evil in its most fundamental mode of operation.

The scope of this book is not to explore all the spiritual dimensions of shame, but to reveal how it shows up in your life in real time and threatens to disrupt the abundant life God intends for you.

> When shame takes hold, it triggers a cascade of intense emotions, self-critical thoughts, and bodily dysregulation.

Shame can destroy your confidence, drain your energy, and defile your self-worth. It is a powerful weapon and can neutralize your desire to love God, yourself, and others well. This weapon has two main settings that the enemy uses to wear you down and eliminate any good or positive influence you might bring into the world.

- *Shame accuses.* The word "accuser" means someone who brings a complaint in a legal case. In Scripture, it says Satan is the one who accuses God's people day and night (Revelation 12:10). Satan relentlessly uses shame to bring accusations against us to convince us of our unworthiness.

- *Shame lies.* Jesus calls Satan the father of lies (John 8:44). The enemy uses the voice of shame to falsely claim that we are not only unworthy but unlovable.

God's explicit strategy to combat the accusations and lies of shame is for people to know his immense and personal love for them (Ephesians 3:17–19), to live in the freedom of that love (Galatians 5:1). Fully loved and free, we are called to get about the business of loving God, ourselves, and others with that kind of love (Mark 12:30–31).

If God's love is so grand and so freely offered, why is shame so effective? Good question. In *The Empire Strikes Back*, young Luke Skywalker asks, "Is the dark side stronger?" Yoda replies, "No, no, no. Quicker, easier, more seductive."

Yoda's description of the dark side reveals how and why shame works. The enemy is not stronger than God, nor are any of the weapons he wields. Shame is his weapon of choice, however, because it is so easy to believe. It's seductive in that the brain, which relies on the efficiency of patterns, falls back on the quickest and easiest story about our worth and lovability. That story, however, is often rooted in our early wounds and losses.

In this ongoing battle between good and evil, we feel the resistance that comes from being caught in the middle. God will not give up on you. He invites you to connection, relationship, and purpose. He will never stop loving you. Satan will never stop trying to convince you that you are unworthy of that love and unfit for that purpose. As Charles Spurgeon wisely said, "Consider how precious the soul must be when both God and the devil are after it."

Clearing the Fog

Our alarm went off at 4:30 a.m. We crawled straight from the bed to our seats in the front of the van, started the engine, and took off driving. This is why I *love* camper van road tripping. Wake up and go.

We were on the South Island of New Zealand, and the next site on our itinerary was the Moeraki Boulders. We heard other travelers talk about the giant spherical rocks that lay on the beach, like a little cluster of prehistoric dinosaur eggs. These boulders are a popular photo spot, and we wanted to get there before sunrise to beat the crowds. Plus, who wouldn't want to sit on a giant, round, mystical boulder to watch the sun come up?

We woke up plenty early but encountered a challenge we hadn't expected: dense fog.

We were on tiny country roads, driving on the left side, navigating S curves and sharp turns, a blanket of heavy white clouds shrouding our view.

Fog slows down travel, making it hard to see the path ahead.

To see the way forward on our soul adventure, we need to clear the fog of confusion about three concepts: shame, guilt, and false guilt. We don't want to fall into the trap of calling everything shame.

Clarity matters. These three distinct emotions can feel similar. To navigate them with wisdom, we must learn to differentiate. We'll look at each in some detail, but one simple way to tell these emotions apart is to listen to the message you're hearing.

Shame says, "I am bad."

Guilt says, "I did something bad."

False guilt says, "I feel badly about how someone else is thinking or feeling, like I did something wrong, but I'm not sure what."

The problem is, sometimes there's so much going on in our lives, it's difficult to hear what's being said.

In 2009, I traveled to Malaysia to spend a week with one of my college besties, Jill, who was living there with her husband and their four young kids. They were working in Penang, a quaint little island off the west coast of the mainland. We hiked with monkeys, went to a traditional Malay wedding, spent time on a Malaysian beach, and shared the deep concerns of our souls until the wee hours of the night.

One of our excursions was to a big city near their home. We did what one must do as a stereotypical American tourist in Asia. We hired a rickshaw. As the driver peddled us around the busy streets, I laughed in delight. The electrifying hubbub jolted my senses. My eyes darted from one bright color to another in the mosaic scenes. New and occasionally pungent smells filled the air.

And oh, the sounds! Street-side vendors called out, motorcycles zoomed, horns blared. The collision of sounds created a symphony of chaos, making it hard to distinguish where each sound originated.

The literature and social media musings discussing shame, guilt, and false guilt can be as noisy as those Malaysian streets, making it hard to distinguish one from the other. My summarized concepts pull from psychology, Scripture, and neuroscience to distill the key differences so you know what you're facing and how to deal with it.

Shame

Shame is a message of flawed personhood, the feeling of not measuring up, a broken identity, a lack of something others have. It is a sense of unworthiness and unlovability.

Do any of these shame statements sound familiar?

- I am not enough.
- I feel unworthy.
- I'm not as disciplined as I should be.
- I'm always such a people-pleaser.
- I should be happier.
- I'm constantly comparing myself to others.
- I should be further along in my spiritual journey.
- I'm not as kind/patient/understanding as I should be.
- I should have achieved more by now.
- I'm not as smart/talented/attractive as others.
- I should be able to do better.

Shame drives disconnection and creates a pattern of negative behavior. If you yell at your child and then say to yourself, "I am a bad mom," shame's accusation sets you up for more self-condemnation, more frustration, more yelling. The experience of shame in the body can be subtle or dysregulating or the combination of both. It can feel like a constant sense of unworthiness or unlovability whirring under the hood. It can also come quickly, causing you to break through your Window of Tolerance.

Watch for shame's vile use of comparison. Anytime you compare your life to someone else's, shame will be lurking around the corner, ready to pounce. Comparison statements often start with the word *should*. It wreaks havoc on the soul when we look at someone else and think, *I should be more like that*. Or *I shouldn't be so* [insert quality of self you don't like]. Social media can be a petri dish for shame because of the barrage of images of perfect lives, perfect people, and easy solutions to complex problems.

As we move through this section, we will address how this unwanted passenger attempts to harm us through accusation, which inevitably leads to feelings of isolation.

Healthy Guilt

Healthy guilt guides us in understanding how we have damaged a relationship, whether that relationship is with God, yourself, or others. It gives us an understanding of sin and how it is damaging. Sin causes a rupture in those relationships; however, Scripture tells us we are not left alone to figure out how we have done damage. I absolutely love this concept in God's Word because it describes the way we receive help as coming from a spiritual "counselor."

In John 16, Jesus hints at his upcoming death. He tells his disciples he will be leaving, all the while assuring his disciples that his departure will turn out to be a good thing for them. In John 16:7, He says he will be sending a *paraklētos* to them. This Greek word is translated as counselor, advocate, helper, or comforter. In other places, Scripture names this as the Spirit. Listen to how the Message version says it, "So let me say it again, this truth: It's better for you that I leave. If I don't leave, *the Friend* won't come. But if I go, I'll send him to you."

A friend! We are given a friend, one who is always available to us. One of this friend's sacred responsibilities is to alert us when we've damaged a relationship. Our souls are formed and shaped by love, so a loving encounter when we have caused harm is what our souls need most. I want to know, in a firm and loving way, when I've caused harm. Don't you?

The voice of that friend will speak firmly but will never condemn (Romans 8:1). Shame goes straight for the jugular of your lovability. The Spirit of God does not attack personhood, dignity, or worthiness. Ever.

Easy translation: I did bad; I am not bad.

Growing up, attending that little white Lutheran church in the middle of a cattle pasture in Arneckeville, I had no idea how honest and powerful the words of the liturgy were, confessing them together and out loud each week. What once felt boring and stale now feels humbling and honest. "We confess that we are captive to sin and cannot free ourselves. We have sinned against you in thought, word, and deed, by what we have done and by what we have left undone. We have not loved you with our whole heart; we have not loved our neighbors as ourselves."

Speaking of confessions and not loving my neighbor . . .

One consistent marriage conflict between Chris and me is when Chris fails to remember plans we previously discussed. We've named it his "innocent bystander" stance, which is a tendency of his to act as if our life is moving along, and I'm the only one who knows the where, what, when, and how of all the moving pieces. I get frustrated when he asks me about plans I'm sure we have *already* talked about. To be fair, I can forget to keep him updated on plans I make.

It's an occurrence that happens frequently enough that we've developed a pattern. He assumes the innocent bystander stance, and I get annoyed quickly and end the conflict by spouting off rudely. (I didn't say it was a healthy pattern.)

If our relationship is going to flourish, it is imperative that I take responsibility for my actions. I know my reactive responses hurts him.

It's wrong and goes against the values I live by which are guided by my understanding of the parameters Scripture gives for healthy, connected relationships. Remember: Healthy boundaries are about knowing and staying true to our values. I value being kind, even when upset, being slow to anger, using words seasoned with grace, and demonstrating self-control in my interactions.

My Friend (the Spirit) tugged at my conscience. I felt guilt (conviction) for my rude behavior toward Chris. I knew I hurt him and offended God in the interaction. That guilt stirred feelings of regret and sadness. Those are uncomfortable feelings. They are also important to the process, guiding me to the path of repentance. *Repentance* simply means turning away from what's wrong and turning toward what's right. What's right is honoring God, Chris, and myself, by seeking to restore our relationship. It's the godly grief Paul wrote about to the church in Corinth when he said, "For the kind of sorrow God wants us to experience leads us away from sin and results in salvation" (2 Corinthians 7:10a, NLT).

Responding to the feeling of healthy guilt, I admit the behavior was wrong. I validate him by acknowledging that my action caused hurt, asking for forgiveness, and seeking restoration. This is how we repair the rupture in our relationship. All the while—through all the uncomfortable feelings of guilt, sadness, and regret—I remain grounded in the reality that I am deeply loved as I am, even when I have done something hurtful.

Whew. This can be intricate stuff, can't it? Let's keep going to understand our final concept.

False Guilt

Paige is thirty-eight and has five children with her husband Ronnie. The focus of Paige's sessions with me has been processing her challenging relationship with her dad. His passive-aggressive behavior has sent a clear message to his adult children: They are expected to be home for Christmas every year regardless of their circumstances. He disregards the complexities of their lives, including work schedules, their own growing families, spouses' families, and financial constraints.

Last year, Paige's family overextended themselves financially and emotionally. She and Ronnie decided to simplify their holiday schedule this year. They determined to set limits on how much they would spend and travel. After talking to her dad to let him know they would not be coming home for Christmas, she told me, "My dad is so upset with me. I feel guilty I'm not going. Maybe we should change our plans. I hate feeling guilty all the time."

What Paige is describing is not healthy guilt, but *false guilt*. Paige has done nothing wrong. She has not acted in a harmful way toward her dad and has not violated any of her core values. She is standing up for them. Remember that false guilt says, "I feel badly about how *someone else* is thinking or feeling." You feel as if you did something wrong, but you didn't.

I said, "Paige, say that again, but this time put the word *false* in front of the *guilt*."

She blinked at me with questions but obliged. "Oh, okay. Hmm. I told Dad our plan, and he is upset with me. I feel *false guilt* I'm not going. Maybe we should change our plans. I hate feeling *false guilt* all the time."

Adding the word *false* in front of the feeling she previously named as guilt enabled her to explore how she feels when her dad is upset with her. She was feeling false guilt about his emotional world. This is big time Hula Hoop work.

In which hula hoop does her dad's upset feeling belong? *His.*

In which hula hoop does Paige and Ronnie's values regarding their financial and emotional limits belong? *Hers.*

With that clarity, she was able to let her dad have his own emotional experience without taking responsibility for it. She was also able to avoid violating her boundaries or expend energy attempting to fix what was not hers to fix. If she were to change her plans because of her dad's challenging emotion, she would be violating her value to make healthy decisions for her own growing family's financial and emotional flourishing. She kindly and clearly offered other options to her dad, but he stayed rigid in his expectation. This was not her responsibility.

I told you that you would need your hula hoops!

The Law of Responsibility is a natural law, like we learned when packing our boundaries. When we live with healthy limits, people in our lives might feel hurt, but they will not be harmed. Paige's dad does not like limits. He will most likely resist them. She and Ronnie made a commitment to their values by limiting their holiday travel, and it is their responsibility to have actionable ways to live out their boundaries.

Paige realized she was resentful of her dad and exhausted by his expectations, not simply because of the pressure he put on her, but because she was not acting in a mature, centered way. Rather than living within her boundaries and gently but firmly resisting his passive-aggressive behaviors, she had been unknowingly carrying the embodied feelings of being a little girl who did not want to upset her dad.

Now that we've cleared the fog of confusion about these three emotions, we can face our unwanted passenger head on. It is not easy to admit when shame shows up. Shame wants nothing more than to keep you quiet, isolated. Keep you pretending.

Oddly enough, I can even feel shame when I admit I have shame.

I have to chuckle at the irony. Every single day, I help people face their shame. I know what it looks like. I know its accusations and lies by heart. And still, I feel it.

We never become completely immune to the tactics of this unwanted passenger, but we can learn to recognize it more quickly when it shows up. That's where we're headed next on our soul adventure. The sooner we shine a light on shame's dark diversions, the more quickly we can take back our lives and experience greater freedom and deeper joy.

Oh! I need to tell you the ending to the story about our foggy morning drive to see those dinosaur-egg-like boulders. We *did* make it to the Moeraki Boulders by sunrise. We were alone on the beach, a bright orange casting its soft glow across the expanse of the water.

Those rocks were some of the craziest, oddest things I have ever seen, mysteriously lying there on the beach as if they had landed there from another world. I was struck with wonder at the experience that was worth every foggy mile it took to get there.

Do the Work

Name something you need to do that you have been avoiding. Face it this week.

Do the Joy

Name one creative thing you enjoy doing. Put it into your schedule this week. Even better, do it with a friend!

9

RUTS THAT KEEP YOU STUCK

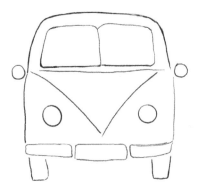

We must run every habit, every thought, every
relationship—everything—through this simple grid:
Does this sow my flesh or my spirit? Will this make
me more enslaved or more free?

—— JOHN MARK COMER ——

I had gotten us into quite a dilemma.

Chris and I were camping through the north island of New Zealand. This trip was our inaugural trip to New Zealand, making it our first experience driving on the left side of the road with a right-sided steering wheel. We felt like amateur teenage drivers. We lacked confidence in every part of the driving experience, having to resist our deeply embedded habits of "regular" driving.

It was my turn to drive. I was backing up the long camper van from a trailhead parking lot. I needed to back up across the road to get into the left lane. As I backed up, I hit the gas too hard. The van lunged backwards. I wanted to release the pressure off the pedal, but it felt like my foot belonged to someone else, lifeless, lying on the pedal like a sandbag. It wouldn't obey me. Because, you know, *physics*. The more I pushed, the further backward we careened. We landed in the ditch directly across from the parking lot we had just left.

We were stuck. The back end of the van was in the ditch, but the front end was nicely straddled across the road. (It's a long van, remember?) I put it in drive and hit the gas pedal. The van didn't budge, although the back tires spun in the ditch. I hit the gas pedal again. Nothing. The more I hit the accelerator, the deeper the rut. The tires continued to spin, now creating a rut they could not escape. Our van was sticking out across the road, a sitting duck for cars coming from either direction.

Stuck in a rut, with me in the driver's seat.

For the next leg of our Soul Adventuring journey, we will be exploring what it means to get stuck in a rut in your life, with you in the driver's seat. In these next bends and twists of our expedition, we will explore the way shame shows up in our behaviors. I call these patterned behaviors *Ruts*.

Ruts represent common ways we get stuck. When tires get stuck in ruts, they do nothing but spin. When they spin, they exert the energy of movement with no forward motion. On this journey of living your brave, joy-filled life, we need to address the ways our tires are spinning, keeping us from making any real movement. Although I knew exactly how the van got stuck, life-ruts often happen without our awareness.

We move in these patterned ways without knowing how we got there or how to stop. Do any of these places of *stuckness* resonate with you?

- trying to please other people
- trying to stay in control
- trying to be perfect
- taking the edge off your day with a glass of wine, scrolling, or binge-watching television

- trying to perform for your worthiness
- feeling like you're not enough
- worrying about upsetting other people

My guess is that, as a member of the human race, you have experienced at least some of those stuck places. I also have a feeling you may not be aware of the way shame is driving those behaviors. Shame, our uninvited, unwanted passenger, seeks to disrupt every soul adventure. I'm inviting you to take an honest look at your life to see patterns that keep you stuck.

Let's flashback to New Zealand, me in the driver's seat, tires spinning.

A few other travelers saw our dilemma and jumped into action. I may or may not have been wailing from the front seat, "Help us! We're stuck! HELP!" One person joined Chris in the ditch to help him push; another directed oncoming traffic to keep us from getting hit. Thanks to the kind assistance from those strangers, we were back on the road in a relatively short time, although each harried moment felt like hours.

I can still feel the panic and embarrassment. Feeling the van lurch backwards, hearing the tires digging deeper ruts, feeling the powerlessness of the spinning tires while straddling the road, doing a royal parade wave from the front seat—even the memory makes me break out in a sweat!

Did you notice how we got out? We didn't get unstuck by ourselves. We needed help. And help showed up. Whether or not you've ever careened a camper van into a ditch in New Zealand, I know you can relate to the awful feeling of getting stuck in a rut. You're not alone. As someone who gets stuck often, I'm here to offer my help, whether you need me to push from the back or direct traffic in the street. God brings the help we need, in the exact way we need it, in the exact time we need it.

Let's have a conversation about how shame shows up in our ruts—so we can get out of them.

Embodied Behaviors

Although Chris and I have lived in two apartments and three homes in our married life, I've only had one childhood home. It remains my parents' home to this day. My parents got married in 1963. Their honeymoon consisted of a one-night stay in a modest motel in Rockport, Texas, an hour down the road from where they both grew up. They came home and moved straight into the new house in Arneckeville they had built during their engagement.

Every stage of my life, from birth to now as a grandma, has been experienced in that place. Even though I haven't lived there since college, it is the same home I grew up in.

Until I was in my late thirties, my parents had a full-length mirror in their bedroom. It was in a perfect spot. There was plenty of room to back up to get that rare *full*-body view. Shoes all the way to hair. You know, the whole enchilada.

I looked in that mirror as a child, teen, college age, and young adult. If that mirror could speak! It witnessed braided pigtails in the 1960s, bell bottoms in the seventies, mighty-fine big hair and shoulder pads in the 80s, mom jeans and babies on my hips in the 90s.

My parents remodeled their bedroom in 2004. The mirror came down, leaving the wall empty where the mirror once hung. It has been gone for more than twenty years, but do you know what I often do when I walk into my parents' room?

I glance at the wall where the mirror used to be. Obviously, I *know* the mirror is no longer there. So why look at the wall for a mirror that is no longer there?

My body holds a long memory of stopping there to look. In my conscious awareness, I *know* the mirror is gone, but my unconscious brain holds an old, implicit memory of the years of looking there. My body holds the memory. In EMDR therapy, these types of automated actions are referred to as an embodied somatic memory, coming from the Latin word *soma*, meaning body. My mirror example is a trivial one. But on the more severe side, a war veteran might drop to the ground when the sound of a car backfiring triggers an embodied somatic memory of the need to be safe from gunfire.

The brain develops ruts for your *protection* to insulate you from feeling something difficult. Your childhood does not have to be one riddled with terrible hurts for you to develop ruts. It is part of the human condition to develop maladaptive patterns along life's path. Some ruts develop in the early years, or they could start later due to an experience in adulthood.

Todd came in to see me to work through his anxiety. He was in his mid-thirties, and he had a strong relationship with his family, with no significant traumas in his life. We explored his story to see if he could put his finger on any early anxieties he may have had as a child. Almost as if he had never really considered it, he recalled being in elementary school when his parents had a lot of conflict with his sister Sheri. She was six years older than he, entering the teen years, and she gave her parents a run for their money. He chuckled warmly as he reflected on how Sheri and his parents tell those stories now.

As a child, however, he was more sensitive. He never wanted to get into trouble. He vividly remembers how, during those years when Sheri was a teenager, he made sure to finish all his chores and get his homework done on time. He figured his parents had enough going on. He didn't want to bother them or get in trouble at school. As the years rolled on, long after the conflict with his sister had died down, he stayed determined to *never* mess up at home or at school. Lying in his bed at night, he did not consciously say to himself, *My parents don't love me, so I need to perform for my worthiness or be perfect.* Those well-worn ruts of performance, worry, and perfectionism were already in place. When he became an adult, those ruts served as a runway for his anxiety.

Todd knew his parents loved him and that he was worthy, yet he had some patterned ways of living his life. I also know the mirror in my parents' room is no longer on the wall. The habits are deeply embedded into relational muscle memory, not consciously chosen. The good news is that once we are aware, we can get busy developing healthier habits!

Identifying Your Ruts

In the list of behavior patterns that follows, the descriptions are written in an exaggerated form. The purpose is to clearly differentiate one from another and precisely identify the embodied habits that keep you stuck.

We'll talk more about this later, but it is important to identify the rut as a *behavior* and not as who you are. If I'm stuck in the rut of Perfectionism, this does not mean I am a Perfectionist. My identity as a human, as someone deeply loved and cherished by God, is deeper and richer than defining myself by a patterned behavior. The verb *stuck* is also important. These are patterned ways we get stuck. If we can figure out where we're stuck, we can get *un*stuck.

Read each of the phrases slowly and without judgment. Pay attention to your body and emotional world, noticing how you feel when you read them. Underline phrases that stand out. Honestly assess yourself and try not to give yourself a low score because you know you shouldn't be that way. We are looking for tendencies. The goal is to bring awareness in order to create new healthy habits. Without spending too much time analyzing the pattern, use the scale of 0–10, where 10 identifies a highest tendency and 0 not at all.

> You can download the Identifying Your Ruts PDF at ChristineWolfHoover.com.

The Rut of Perfection

My life is marked by getting it right. I don't give myself permission to fail. If I do, I beat myself up. I stay frustrated with myself for my flaws. I hustle for my worthiness. I am an all-or-nothing kind of person. I have exacting standards for myself and others. When something goes wrong, I ruminate about what I should have changed and do not let myself off the hook. I can procrastinate for fear of not getting it right. When I procrastinate, I feel bad for my lack of effort and feel guilty. I often feel uptight and driven.

Scale 0–10: _____

The Rut of People Pleasing

I avoid upsetting or disappointing others, even at the cost of speaking up for myself. I want people to know what I want without having to ask. I crave acceptance. Keeping the peace is my job. I don't know who I am if I'm not taking care of others. I love to serve, but I can secretly feel resentful if I'm not seen or if others are not grateful for all I do. I feel the need to justify myself, and I often rehearse how I will explain my decisions to other people. Other's opinions and preferences seem to matter more than mine. I get exhausted from always wondering what others are thinking of me. I often feel weary.

Scale 0–10: _____

The Rut of Scarcity

I'm constantly aware of things I don't have enough of: time, money, energy, experiences, relationships. Making mistakes brings a deep sense of not-*enoughness*. I can overcompensate and then feel like I'm too much. I hoard my energy and resources, afraid there is not enough for another time. I can be threatened by others' success and flourishing. I have a nagging sense I should have done more. I am intolerant of my weakness. I resist receiving or asking for help because it reveals I don't have what it takes. I often feel less-than.

Scale 0–10: _____

The Rut of Performance

I am what I do. If I slow down, I feel lazy. I try to prove to myself and others that I am a hard, diligent worker. I fear failure, so I work harder. I can be overly concerned about presenting an image of success. I have a deep, yet secret, need to be better than others. Even in my spiritual life, I feel the need to prove to God and others I have it together.

My identity is intertwined with my job, my family, my successes, or failures. I tend to value achievement over relaxation. I care deeply how I am perceived by others. I often feel exhausted.

Scale 0–10: _____

The Rut of Numbing

Life's pressures feel too much. I want to be seen as someone who handles life well. My go-to escape mechanisms (shopping, drinking, working, binging on TV, gaming, planning, eating, not eating, scrolling, solving other people's problems, etc.) help me disconnect, taking the edge off the stress. Finding relief is what matters. My emotions seem intolerable, especially the darker feelings. I get exhausted from life's never-ending demands pressing in on me. When I numb, I convince myself it isn't a big deal or as bad as other vices. I hide my behavior, making a myriad of excuses. I often feel regretful.

Scale 0–10: _____

The Rut of Control

I can have unrealistic expectations of myself and others, leading to criticism and dissatisfaction. I can be resistant to change and have difficulty compromising. I stay in control to protect myself and others. It is hard for me to delegate tasks or responsibilities, needing to be in charge and have things my way. I tend to come up with unsolicited solutions to other people's problems, attempting to rescue, control, or micromanage. I am a black-and-white thinker. Life's complexities are best handled the way I do things. The world can be full of threats, and I must protect myself (and my family) from those perceived dangers. I often feel afraid.

Scale 0–10: _____

The Rut of Worry

I have a hard time relaxing and being in the present moment, my mind thinking of the next thing. I replay past incidents as well as future events. I attempt to seek near-perfect solutions to problems, fearing I will make the wrong decision. I think of lies or excuses to tell people when I am afraid they will be upset with me. My anxiety often manifests in an obsessive need to plan and control schedules. After I make it through something tough, I wonder why I worried about it the way I did. I ruminate on potential problems and negative outcomes. I often feel anxious.

Scale 0–10: _____

Insight is the first step toward change. We cannot heal what we do not first acknowledge. We must name it. Identifying the shame ruts keeping you stuck empowers you to develop the new embodied habits that will get you moving instead of just spinning your wheels.

The Unstuck Life

A few years ago, Chris and I went on one of our most memorable trips ever—wild camping in Costa Rica. I say wild camping because it was truly *wild*. We rented a Toyota FJ Cruiser with a tent on top and drove all around Costa Rica, camping on beaches for free, camping near volcanoes and in locals' front yards. Crazy, I know!

One late afternoon, we found a place to park and camp off a main road on the edge of a lake. Looking down at the campsite from the road, it seemed at first like a quaint little cove at the bottom of the hill. We drove down the bumpy hill, the road more like a dirt trail than a real road. We parked on a little dirt peninsula. It was pleasant enough. Just as I was pulling out the camp stove to start dinner, a thunderstorm quickly blew in. It was a doozy. We were now in a torrential downpour with no shelter from the rain. We quickly packed up the cooking gear, our raincoats useless against the storm. With all the rain, we began to feel insecure about the dirt peninsula. Our camping spot was quickly morphing from dirt to mud. It wasn't so quaint anymore. We needed to get out of there.

We hurriedly jumped in the FJ, soaking wet. It was a messy, uncomfortable drive up and out, but we made it. Shout out to the 4-wheel drive! It took several miles for all the mud to finally sling off the tires. Chris drove while I looked on the phone for other campsites. Not much luck. We finally found a youth hostel and wondered if we could camp in their parking lot. Chris ran in to ask while I searched the map for other possibilities.

Chris came back smiling, with a hopeful shrug in his shoulders. They said no to camping in their parking lot, but they had a canvas tent already set up. We could stay in it for $17. It was getting dark and $17? Win/Win.

This was more than a win. He had hit the jackpot, baby! Our meager $17 landed us in a stunning canvas glamping tent perched high in the jungle, with a secluded walkway to a cute front porch. Inside, a gorgeous bed was draped with a fabric canopy. We even had a closet! But the real surprise was the bamboo deck off the back that jetted out into the trees. We had our own private jungle overlook.

Once we settled in, we sat for hours on that deck, feet propped up on the bamboo rails. It seemed as if God had designed this jungle sanctuary purely for our enjoyment. We spotted the monkeys swinging and making their noises in the trees, watched the lightning light up the sky, listened to the symphony of bird calls, all the while sheltered under the awning. It was the most magical night of our entire trip.

I want you to take a moment to see the contrast:

> the dirty, muddy, potholed peninsula in the pouring rain
> *versus*
> the vibrant sounds and sights of life in the jungle.

Can you see and feel the difference in your mind's eye? This is the contrast available to us in the process of getting unstuck. It reminds me of Jesus's succinct warning and promise in John, telling us the enemy wants to destroy our lives, but God wants to provide us with life, abundant life, life to the fullest.[8] That is a soul adventuring promise if I've ever heard one! The offer of abundance instead of destruction. The promise of life instead of death. Muddy roads with potholes where we can stay stuck or vibrant sights and sounds where we can enjoy life.

Getting unstuck will require some grit. But I know you are not afraid of a little hard work.

Are you ready?

Do It to Get Unstuck

You've probably seen the iconic Bob Newhart video where he counsels a woman terrified of being buried alive in a box. He hilariously yells his two words of advice to her: "Stop it!" If you haven't seen it, go look it up. It's a classic.

Our first strategy is almost as simplistic as his advice. One of the primary ways to get unstuck is to find the behavior that keeps you stuck—and then do the opposite. Do a new thing. The new action creates new healthy habits.

Instead of *Stop it*, let's *Do It!*

Let me explain.

Since habits are not a function of our logical brain, it won't help to tell yourself what you should or shouldn't do. "Shoulds" don't work.

I *should* stop trying to be perfect.

I *should* exercise more.

I *should* stop worrying about what middle school will be like for our son.

I *should* not care what my coworkers think of me.

I *should* stop drinking so much.

I *should* stop obsessing about my child's problems.

Embodied habits require embodied change. We need to do and feel something new to build the new habit. We are implementing the wheat field example from Chapter Four when we learned how the

---

8   John 10:10

brain builds new habits. The *Do It* strategy involves having mindful awareness of the emotional and behavioral challenge and then moving and feeling your way through to the new habit.

When Todd came to see me about his anxiety, we discovered the rut of performance. It didn't work to say, "I know I should not feel lazy when I slow down." He had to do something different. Here is what *Do It* looked like for Todd:

> **Rut**: Performance
>
> **Behavior/Emotion**: If I slow down, I feel lazy.
>
> **Do It (new behavior, new emotions, new self-talk)**: I will leave my laptop at work three days a week. On those evenings, I will do something I enjoy. I do not have to perform for my worthiness. When the feelings of laziness come up, I will practice deep breathing and I will move my body. I will allow myself to feel the discomfort. I will remind myself I am learning new habits to live a healthier, more balanced life.

Todd is walking down a new path in the wheat field, one small practice at a time. But he doesn't have to do it alone. Remember when we got stuck in the ditch in New Zealand? We got out of the ditch because people helped us out. The *Do It* strategy is helpful to practice with other people. Tell a friend you want to practice some new habits. Name a rut and one specific part you want to work on. Break it down specifically, like Todd and I did. Talk about what it was like when you practiced the new behavior. Follow up as you continue to grow and when you get stuck again.

This practice can also be used as a prayer time. Since God is an always available, always loving, relational being, we can reach toward Him. Change happens when we are anchored in love. We must be able to experience our value and worth, our lovability, distinctly separate from how we perform or show up in the world. God offers his unconditional, unlimited love—a love that is wider and longer and higher and deeper than anything we can fathom.[9] It is a love big enough for all of us.

For my rut of scarcity, I named and completed my *Do It* strategy. I then turned it into a prayer. Here is what that sounded like:

> **Rut**: Lord, I admit I struggle with scarcity. Forgive me for thinking I don't have enough when you have promised to give me everything I need.
>
> **Behavior/Emotion**: Father, I see how self-sufficient I can be because it is hard to ask for help. Thank you for showing me how weak I feel. I know weakness is not a bad thing.
>
> **Do It (new behavior, new emotions, new self-talk)**: When I called my friend to ask for help with the situation, it felt hard. Thank you for helping me through that. I know reaching for friendship is not neediness; it is healthiness. I am creating a new, healthier habit in my soul, learning how to be interdependent in my relationships, bringing new freedom and new joy. Thank you for the people you've provided for me. Thank you for providing abundantly and immeasurably more than I can ask or imagine. Guide me to walking in new ways of wholeness. Help me experience the truth that I am complete and whole in you. I am enough in you.

I'm going to pull a Bob Newhart on you! *Stop it* on the shoulds! Time to practice new behaviors to get out of old ruts. Time to *Do It*! Practicing new ways of acting and feeling will be hard at first. Keep in mind the difference between the muddy, potholed road and the vibrant jungle sounds. The *Do It* strategy is about naming and practicing new ways of moving in your world, which is a pathway to an abundant life instead of a stuck life.

---

9 Ephesian 3:17–19

Pick Up Grace to Get Unstuck

The first time I introduced the concept of shame ruts to anyone beyond my clients was from the stage at a Christian women's conference. I had painstakingly prepared my presentation and felt proud of the work I had done. I'm usually a wing-it kind of speaker, but for this conference I had deliberately practiced the delivery many times. When it was go time, I was ready!

I walked onto the stage after my introduction to put my notes on the podium, a few things happening differently than I expected. First, I accidentally brought my phone with me, so I simply placed it on the podium. My-way-too-big Bible, plus my notes, plus the phone, made the space feel crowded and my notes hard to see. It wasn't a huge deal, but I felt off balance, a little off my game. I bumbled the beginning and made a joke that fell flat. I eventually got in the groove, recentering myself after the first couple of shaky minutes. Overall, I felt good about the session and the way the audience engaged with and connected to the content.

But guess what? As soon as I stepped down off the stage, the ruminating began. *I should have done the intro better. I should have been more prepared. Why did I take my stupid phone up there? I'm embarrassed that I told that dumb joke about my kids.*

You're catching the irony, right?

I had just finished teaching about shame ruts, and my proverbial rut-making wheels were spinning before I even took my seat.

Recognizing shame at work, I knew what to do. I needed to pick up some manna.

Exodus 16 is where we first read about manna in the Bible. God had rescued his people from slavery in Egypt by delivering them through the miraculous parting of the Red Sea. The Israelites were a month and a half into their epic journey, making their way across the scorching desert to the land God had promised them. Talk about a soul adventure!

No one enjoyed this part of the journey, however. They were hungry. They were angry at Moses and Aaron for dragging them out into the desert where they felt lost. After walking for a month and a half and probably not getting a whole lot of sleep in their overcrowded campsites, I bet they were tired. *Hungry. Angry. Lost. Tired.* HALT. I warn my clients to be mindful about their emotional reactivity when these four emotions show up, especially all at the same time. It's no wonder the Israelites were feeling frustrated and grumpy.

They started complaining, longing for the comforts of home. You know, back in slavery. Super comfortable. Instead of giving them what they asked for, God gave them what they needed. He dropped manna (a type of bread from heaven) on the ground to feed his people. He provided exactly enough for each day. Their only job was to gather. That word *gather* is repeated over and over in this passage of Scripture.

I didn't need anything to eat when I stepped down off that stage, but I did need something that only God could provide. I had some gathering to do. I needed to remind myself that I had exactly what I needed.

Gathering what we need, in each and every moment, is an important strategy for getting unstuck.

I felt myself disconnecting from who God tells me I am and slipping into my go-to ruts of perfectionism, performance, and scarcity. I visualized myself reaching down and picking up my manna, God's provision for me. Some provisions I pick up regularly are wisdom, comfort, kindness, God's loving presence, grace, joy, a calming of my unsettled spirit, and love for others. Picking up manna is the way I practice, in an embodied way, bringing me back to myself, back to my *enoughness* in that moment.

As I took my seat, I took a deep breath, slowing down my body and centering myself. I imagined bending down to pick up the grace I needed in the moment. I gathered my provisions, then touched my heart and looked up and smiled, as if seeing his pleasure for me. I opened my palms to symbolize receiving his love into my body. As I touched my heart again, I told myself how deeply God loved me—as

I am, in my present state, mistakes and all. I asked God to fill me with his delight. In my mind, I saw a God who enjoys me, no matter how I perform or what I do.

My heart settled; the rut-carving ruminating ceased. Shame was no longer in control as I engaged with women in attendance afterward. I even allowed myself to genuinely receive their words of encouragement without drawing attention to my perceived mistakes.

I can teach about shame ruts *and* experience them.

You will learn to identify your ruts, and they will continue to show up. Don't be discouraged. This is why we need an abundance of grace, moment by moment. You, too, can get unstuck by pausing and picking up the grace you need. Jesus promises to provide. He says, "I am the bread of life. Whoever comes to me will never go hungry, and whoever believes in me will never be thirsty" (John 6:35, NIV). The supplies you need are available. All you have to do is gather.

Watch Your Language

It matters how we talk about the ruts. One of the most dangerous things we can do is make our ruts our identity.

I am a perfectionist.

I'm a worrier.

I'm a people pleaser.

I am a procrastinator.

The language of permanence solidifies a pattern as an identity. Philosophy professor and Christian writer Dallas Willard said, "It is human nature to resist deep inward change, for such change threatens our sense of personal identity." When we adopt a pattern as our identity, there is then no need or opportunity to work on changing the pattern, because it is named as a permanent part of our personality.

Making sense of behavioral patterns is different than defining yourself by them. Name your ruts, but don't name yourself *by* your ruts.

Maybe you have called yourself a people-pleaser for as long as you remember. Maybe you excelled in sports or had incredible academic successes, so you call yourself a perfectionist. Maybe you joke about being a shopaholic or a workaholic.

Name your ruts, but don't name yourself *by* your ruts.

I'm really picky about this. When anyone tells me, "I'm a perfectionist. That's just how I am." I stop them dead in their tracks and say, "Nope. Don't define yourself like that. Practice saying, 'I tend to move toward perfectionism when I am feeling _____.'"

I tend to move toward people pleasing when...

I tend to move toward scarcity when . . .

I tend to move toward performance when . . .

Practice this week. When a rut shows up, get curious about what got your wheels spinning. It could be a feeling or a situation or a certain relationship that triggers you to move in a patterned way. There is so much growth available when you use the "soft and slow, curious and kind" emotional strategies. This is not a one-time exploration. This soul adventuring strategy needs to be a part of your life, for the rest of your life.

There's more to this practice of acknowledging your true identity. We'll get there, but first, we need to expose the final strategy shame uses to sabotage our great adventure.

Do the Work

List the two ruts with the highest numbers. Be on the watch for them this week. Notice what is happening in those situations.

Do the Joy

Name one person you enjoy being around. Reach toward them today to let them know you appreciate their presence in your life.

10

ROADBLOCKS

The worst lies are the lies we tell ourselves.

——————— RICHARD BACH ———————

After a two-week camping trip through Maine and Nova Scotia, our camper van was due back at the rental lot in downtown Jersey City, New Jersey, by 10:30 a.m. We were on the cusp of being charged an extra day rental fee if we didn't return in the next thirty minutes.

We had expected traffic. I mean, it is Jersey City, New Jersey. The name alone sounds *trafficky*. But the snarl we were stuck in seemed out of control. Horns honking, people yelling, cars scurrying this way and that, crawling in every direction, piling up on back streets.

After a relaxing vacation, it felt like being punched in the face, the stress jolting us back to reality. What was the deal with the traffic? On a Saturday morning? We could not figure it out.

Until we hit the roadblock.

We looked up to see two stern-faced police officers standing in the middle of a street, angrily blowing their whistles. They glared at us through our giant windshield. Behind them, the street was barricaded. In their rough New Jersey way, they barked at us (please try your best to hear this in a Jersey accent), "What the hell you doin' on dis street? Git outta here. Turn around!" They continued blowing their whistles, impatiently motioning for us to turn around.

What was happening? Why was there a barrier? We refocused our eyes to look again. Then we saw it.

In the street in front of us, we spotted a long stretch of weary runners pounding the pavement, crowds cheering them on.

It was a marathon.

We had unknowingly turned down a barricaded street and driven directly up to the runners. I mean, right up to them. The police officers were the only objects keeping us from driving onto the marathon course.

Lines of cars were parallel parked on both sides of the tiny street, and there was a roadblock in front of us. Our van seemed as large as a double-decker bus in London.

Trapped with no way forward. That's what roadblocks do. They can stop us dead in our tracks.

Shame can do the very same thing. Block our path forward.

That annoying unwanted passenger can create ruts *and* roadblocks.

Shame ruts keep you stuck in patterned behaviors, especially if you believe the lie that those behaviors are who *you* are. (*I am a people pleaser. I am a perfectionist. I am a procrastinator.*)

Shame roadblocks can also prevent you from living out your soul adventures, but in a slightly different way. Roadblocks are stories you unknowingly tell yourself about your unworthiness, stories you hold in your body about being unworthy of love and belonging. They are the dark voices of shame, voices like *I'm not enough. I am a disappointment. I am too much. I am all alone. I'm not lovable. I always let people down.*

These stories block our bravery and hinder our joy. We must face them and then find a way around shame's ploy to stop us dead in our tracks.

For now, let's go back to New Jersey, with those red-faced, whistle-blowing police officers. Chris made a daring and miraculous three-point turn on that tiny street without hitting anything or anyone, but there was no way to make it to the rental agency on time. Every road was blocked. We were *stuck*.

But not really.

We made a quick call to the rental agency, informing them we couldn't get there, and we would *not* be paying the extra day rental charge. The employees had been blocked from getting to work as well, so grace abounded. We suddenly had three bonus hours of vacation time in Jersey City. Nothing lights my fire like the chance to have a little unplanned fun! It was time to turn lemons into lemonade, roadblocks into adventures.

First off, we weren't mad at the runners for blocking our way, so we decided to have a little fun celebrating them. Hooray for celebrating! We found a spot on the race route and cheered on a few random, exhausted runners. They looked up at us, miserable and ragged, but grinned, nonetheless. Heck, who doesn't love a random cheering section every now and then?

Far removed from the stress of the traffic chaos, we strolled and shopped down a cute little New Jersey street, grabbed lunch, taking the time to reminisce about our trip. After a while, we noticed that the marathon was winding down. The roads were opening up, so we made our way back to the van.

I stepped into one final shop. Sitting on a shelf by the door, I saw a souvenir I absolutely had to have. I knew it was God's way to remind me of this day. It was a half-inch-thick wooden block about the size of a business card. Colorful cross-stitching thread wove through the front and back, forming an arrow. Below the arrow, the word *GO* was stamped in white. This sweet little block sits on my desk as a clear reminder that roadblocks are not dead ends.

They are passageways to new hope. To a new direction. To go. To go a new way.

Okay, soul adventurer, let's face some roadblocks. Onward to find our way through the barricades to discover a passageway to lives filled with more bravery and joy.

The Stories We Tell

I was alone on a walk in my neighborhood, mentally working through a tough situation from earlier in the day. Our neighborhood is a tranquil place to work through hard things. Towering pines rise majestically from the ground, offering a protective sanctuary yet leaving enough room for the sky to peek through. Tears gently streamed down my cheeks. My lips trembled.

Suddenly, a piercing voice echoed between the houses and trees. It was more of a scream than a shout. "Christine can make MISTAKES! Christine CAN make mistakes! CHRISTINE CAN MAKE MISTAKES!"

The intensity startled me, especially when I realized the scream had escaped out of my own vocal cords. It was a guttural, spontaneous release of emotion, emerging from a deep place in my soul.

When I say screamed, I mean, I *screamed*! It was loud. I threw both of my hands straight up in the air. The tears intensified.

The neighbors must've been worried.

Earlier in the day, I had a phone call with our youngest son, Colton. He was twenty-five at the time. We had accomplished the monumental feat of engaging in a grown-up conversation about a recent hurtful encounter between us. He let me know how I hurt him by something I had said. I remained open and non-defensive during our conversation. I was able to hear him and take responsibility. It was a productive conversation. I told him how much courage it took to call me, showing such vulnerability. I was proud of us both for navigating it maturely. We ended with a mutual and sincere, "I love you so much." I hit the red end-call button, feeling great about the chat.

Until I didn't.

As the day progressed, I grew increasingly frustrated with myself over the offhand comment I had made that caused the hurt in the first place. Regret, like flammable gas, saturated the memory of my words, igniting new accusations. All on repeat, looping over and over in my head like a hamster wheel spinning out of control.

You've been there, right? Rumination tainted with a tiny drop of toxic accusation about your worthiness or your character. This is a shame roadblock. Why do we do this? Why do we say and feel things about ourselves that are hurtful and damaging? The answer is complicated, but let's simplify it so we can make it practical.

The brain does not like unfinished story loops; it wants a full story. The savvy writers of binge-worthy shows know we are wired for story. It's that craving that keeps us clicking for the next episode. I'm embarrassed to admit how lightning fast I binge-watched *Breaking Bad*. It felt like *I had to* click to the next episode. We desperately want to know what happens next. We are wired for resolution. We are meaning makers.

When we are hooked by big emotions or in the throes of a relational disconnection, the brain attempts to make meaning of the situation and grab the quickest story it can find. Our brains are efficient, wanting to use as little energy as possible. In Chapter 5, we explored how our stories shape our brain. Our ancient stories and attachment wounds are held in our implicit memories, still cycling in our stories today. Since the amygdala has been online since birth, it is saturated in experiential learning. It remembers every fear, every insecurity, and it tosses up those stories whenever we feel threatened today.

Since our unwanted passenger, shame, has been with us all along, it finds a way to quickly finish the story loop. Feelings of unworthiness and unlovability, which the enemy put into play from earlier experiences, are intermingled, creating a story resolution. Watch how quickly this can happen:

The situation: My partner broke up with me.
The quick story: I am not good enough. I knew it.
Story resolution complete.

The situation: My adult child is having problems in their life.
The quick story: It's all my fault.
Story resolution complete.

The situation: I wasn't invited to the gathering at a friend's house.
The quick story: I'm always forgotten. I've never mattered.
Story resolution complete.

The situation: After my sales pitch, the client cancelled the contract and went with the competitor.
The quick story: Of course this happened. I always fall short.
Story resolution complete.

Do you see how fast this can work without our awareness? Roadblocks are the fastest stories your brain can provide when hooked by a big emotion or by a challenging circumstance. The accusations shoot out in rapid succession as your brain works at lightning speed to finish the story. Some stories are even carried through the generations, passed down implicitly. They are embodied ways of feeling about your identity and worth.

Soul adventurer, are you weary of the feeling you didn't do enough, you are not enough, you are broken, you are unlovable? Let's start a revolution against this unwanted passenger! Let's not let it rob us of the beautiful adventure God has set out for us.

Identifying Your Roadblocks

As with the Identifying Your Ruts, this is not a thinking exercise; it's a feeling exercise. Tune in to your body as you read the following statements. Pay attention to what you feel as you read. Don't judge what you should or should not feel. Your body will let you know what roadblocks are stored in your body. Circle the phrases[10] that activate emotions and sensations. It might feel like a gentle head nod with the words *Yes, yes I feel that way sometimes.* Take your time. These words can be painful to read, stirring up deeply held pain. If it feels too hard right now, that's okay. You can come back later. If you don't want to mark in your book, a PDF is available at ChristineWolfHoover.com.

Worthiness Roadblocks

It is not okay to be me.

I am damaged.

I am worthless.

I should be better.

I feel inadequate, especially
  compared to…

I am insignificant.

I don't matter.

I'm not good enough.

I am too much.

I am the wrong kind of person.

I should always have it
  all together.

Relational Roadblocks

I am unworthy of love.

I am unwanted.

I am unimportant.

I'm not as smart/talented/suc-
  cessful as others.

I am all alone.

I am not lovable.

I am a disappointment.

I can't show weakness. I must
  show others I am okay.

Responsibility Roadblocks

It's my fault.

I must not be a burden.

I should be able to do better.

I have to do it all.

I should be more disciplined.

I am not allowed to
  make mistakes.

I am a failure.

I am lazy. I should work harder.

---

10 These are adapted negative cognitions from the EMDR therapy protocol.

Safety Roadblocks

I am helpless.

I am in danger.

I am voiceless.

I should not be so scared.

I am not safe.

I am not in control.

I am powerless.

I am hopeless.

It's not okay for me to feel.

I can't stand up for myself.

Character Roadblocks

I should have known better.

I always let people down.

I should be happier and
more successful.

I am broken.

I don't matter.

I don't have what it takes.

I am stupid.

I can't trust myself.

I don't measure up.

I am weak.

Did you notice any themes in categories? Be gentle with yourself if you circled numerous statements. It's okay. Like the ruts, we cannot change what we have not named. The purpose is to be aware of when and how they show up, providing you important information to help get past the roadblocks barring your way to living a braver and more joy-filled life.

Staying Strong Against the Winds of Shame

As you review your roadblocks, notice how the statements drip with accusation. Can you see the condemnation oozing out of them? Roadblocks are destructive to our souls because they are sending dark messages of a flawed personhood, a sense of not being okay.

I wish rewriting shame stories and busting through roadblocks would happen easily. I wish we could simply say the opposite and be done. Since shame has dark origins, it requires more than a simple solution. Let's talk about how to push back against the accusations.

The statements are not simply thoughts we can pull out of our heads like I pluck olives off my pizza. We can't open our brains, take out the statement *I don't matter*, drop in an *I do matter* statement, and be on our merry way. Because the roadblocks are deeply intertwined with our feelings, our sense of self, and our personhoods, they need an embodied solution. A slower, more grounded solution.

A fascinating experiment in the early 1990s called Biosphere 2 was conducted by a research facility in Arizona investigating Earth's living systems. The researchers built a dome and created an artificial ecosystem within it. I remember when terrariums were a trend in the seventies, and everyone had cool glass jars with little plants growing in them. Biosphere 2 was essentially a life-size terrarium. The goal of the experiment was to explore innovative agricultural practices without harming the planet. Researchers discovered an interesting problem with the Biosphere 2's trees. They noticed that trees grew faster in the dome than those in natural environments. It was when they reached maturity that the problem became apparent. The trees fell down. Over and over again, seemingly healthy trees just fell over. The researchers were puzzled. What was happening?

The answer surprised the researchers. They had designed the artificial world of the dome to mimic nature. It had light, rain, soil, everything—except wind. When the researchers studied the fallen trees more carefully, they noticed two things. The trees had shallow roots and were missing an outer layer of bark known as stress wood. Both of these important features strengthen trees and help them stand tall.

Guess what develops stress wood?

Wind!

No wind = no stress. No stress = no strength.

Without the stress of the wind pushing against the trees, they grew quickly and never developed the strength of deep roots and stress wood necessary to sustain that growth. Here's the bottom line: The trees needed the right amount of stress pushing against them to become strong. The very winds that could topple the trees are the same winds that strengthen their roots and build strong bark.

This is our strategy against the shame roadblocks.

The winds of accusation that could stop us dead in our tracks are the very winds that can strengthen us and set us free.

> The winds of accusation that could stop us dead in our tracks are the very winds that can strengthen us and set us free.

Deep Roots. Strong Backs.

Remember when we talked in Chapter 6 about how facing emotion is like swimming toward the sharks? What I'm proposing here is similar. The trees in the biosphere needed the wind to develop resilience. To fight the roadblocks, I'm going to teach you to face the wind.

Let's say you made a significant mistake at work. It's been a busy season without much extra time to take care of yourself. You've had a hard day, and your patience reservoir is low. After you realized you made the mistake, you scrolled on social media. With all those factors in place, you are *perfectly* set up for a barrage of shame accusations to start rapid firing.

You begin to say statements to yourself like, *What's wrong with me? I am such an idiot. I never get it right. Classic me, always making mistakes.*

First, I want you to notice something. The shame accusations aren't the exact phrases from our list; they are bits and pieces of them. The accusations will flow from your brain with your language and from your story. The list of roadblocks is only a starting point to help you identify the generalities of those types of statements.

A couple of years ago, I was in a challenging season of emotional struggle. One morning I woke up feeling especially down. A combination of factors made me particularly vulnerable to shame. I journaled my feelings to tease out the accusations. Look at all the different iterations and combinations of roadblocks that came up for me:

It feels like I'm the wrong kind of person. I don't feel like I'm enough. I feel like I have a flaw that can't be fixed. I don't feel like I ever work hard enough. I don't do enough. I'm not kind enough. Thoughtful enough. Considerate enough. Not a good enough gift giver. Not a good enough artist. Not a good enough grandma. Not as creative as other people. Not as fun. I can't even write a stupid book I said I would write. I've made too many mistakes. I see so much wrong with how I've done life.

It's hard for me to even read those words. I do not feel that way about myself very often. The accusations were intense that day, but my roots were strong. And here I am, writing the stupid book I couldn't write. *Hah!* Take that, you worthless unwanted passenger!

Speaking of strong. Let's get back to the wind and trees and build shame resilience so we can build deep roots and strong backs. This practice may sound counter-intuitive, but it is a powerful antidote to shame.

We will practice befriending shame, meaning we are not freaking out when it shows up. It is important to accept that shame will be with us. Harriett Lerner, psychologist and author says it this way, "The real culprits are our knee jerk responses to shame. Acting courageously when shame enters the picture requires extraordinary courage because people will do anything to escape from shame."

Let's get started:

Take a few deep breaths. Now imagine yourself as a tree. You are sturdy, strong. Feel your feet, solid on the ground. At your shoulders, you have branches reaching high up to take in the sunshine. Take a few deep breaths in and out. Envision your feet with roots, going deep into the ground. Imagine your back as the trunk of a tree. See it as strong, sturdy. As you breathe, say to yourself, *I am deeply rooted. I am grounded. I am strong.* As you breathe and say those phrases, feel the sturdiness in your body.

Now imagine the winds of shame blowing at you, using the phrases you circled on your list. You can see the wind moving the branches, attempting to push you over. Maybe you can even envision a specific, shame-inducing situation attempting to blow you over. See yourself as you stay grounded against the wind. Your back is steady, your roots are deep.

The wind blows through your branches, but you are strong. You are solid.

Respond by speaking truth to yourself:

- I know shame wants me to believe . . . (Use the shame road-block phrases you circled.)
- Of course, I feel those things because of . . . (Insert the part of your story that makes you vulnerable to those accusations.) My body is simply remembering old stories of hurt. I can let my body remember while I stay strong.
- I know the accusations feel true in my body. I can feel the sadness and frustration. (Name other emotions of the accusations.) I can let the wind blow over but not blow me over. My roots are deep; my back is strong.

You have endured the wind. Your roots are deeper and your back is stronger. After allowing the accusations to blow, kindly tell yourself the truth about your God-given sense of worthiness and lovability. Use the list of Freedom Stories in the Appendix. They are statements of truth about you. This is also a great time to add in scripture references about who you are in Christ. You can say something like . . .

- I know those accusations felt true, but I faced them and made it through. I don't need to fear those feelings. I can grow stronger as I withstand the wind. God tells me there is no condemnation in Christ Jesus (Romans 8:1).

- I know I am worthy, enough, safe. It's okay to be me. God says I am fully loved and accepted, as I am, in this moment. Nothing I can do can make him love me more or love me less.
- I am strong. I will not be blown over.

A couple of scriptures that can remind you that you will not be blown over include . . .

> So then, just as you received Christ Jesus as Lord, continue to live your lives in him, your roots grow down into him, and let your lives be built on him.
>
> —Colossians 2:6–7, NIV

> But we have this treasure in jars of clay to show that this all-surpassing power is from God and not from us. We are hard pressed on every side, but not crushed; perplexed, but not in despair; persecuted, but not abandoned; struck down, but not destroyed.
>
> —2 Corinthians 4:7–9, NIV

> Cast your cares on the Lord and he will sustain you; he will never let the righteous be shaken.
>
> —Psalms 55:22, NIV

As we close out the exercise, take a few deep breaths, noticing your feet, feeling how strong and sturdy they are. Imagine deeper roots growing off your feet as you finish, keeping you from blowing over. Remind yourself how the winds made you stronger. Feel your core and your back as strong and steady, knowing the accusations blew right past. You had the fortitude to feel them but not be blown over. Say something to yourself like, *I faced shame. It feels true and powerful, but it is not. I am still standing. My roots are deeper; my back is stronger.*

This exercise is not a one-time practice. I want you to build it into your life. The beauty of the imagination God gave you is that you can access it anytime, anywhere. You can be in the front seat of your car with screaming kids in the backseat. You can be in the classroom with test anxiety destroying your sense of self. You can be walking out of the church service, feeling all alone and unseen. Anywhere you go, you can fight the winds of shame with the beautiful gift of a sanctified imagination, bringing goodness and peace into your mind and body.

Instead of avoiding shame, we have learned how to face it. Instead of screaming back at it, we have taken away its power by letting it blow through our branches. We have deep roots and a strong back. The very winds of accusation that tried to stop us dead in our tracks are the same winds that are now strengthening us and setting us free.

I think it's time for us to do a loud *Braveheart*, William Wallace shout out: "FREEDOM!"

Our Souls Are Changed by Love

The last defining mark of our unwanted passenger is its ability to bring isolation and the sense of being all alone. Curt Thompson says, "I am not just sad, angry, or lonely. But ultimately these feelings rest on the bedrock that I am alone with what I feel, and no one is coming to my aid. Shame undergirds other affective states because of its relationship to being left alone." To be human is to need relationships. When we learned about the relational brain, we discovered how terrifying aloneness is for our neural networks. Heck, aloneness is bad for every single part of us.

How do we fight the aloneness of shame? With love.

Shame shrivels when love shows up.

In the Harry Potter series, Harry's scar represents a beautiful story arc about unconditional love. Voldemort killed Harry's parents, James and Lily, while trying to murder Harry as a baby. Lily's sacrificial love blocked the killing curse from Harry, leaving the lightning bolt scar on his forehead. Dumbledore told Harry, "It was because of your mother, Harry. She sacrificed herself for you. That kind of act leaves a mark. Not a mark on your body, but on your soul."

Shame shrivels when love shows up.

We can leave a mark on each other when we realize the power of love. It is God's greatest and strongest weapon. I learned these four important phrases from James K.A. Smith in his books, *Desiring the Kingdom* and *You Are What You Love:*

We are lovers, not learners.

We are feelers not thinkers.

We are formed, not informed.

We are loved into new ways of loving.

These phrases added more depth and beauty to the trauma work I had been doing with clients. The words clarified a foundational truth on which I had staked my claim: Relational wounds are healed in relationship. We cannot think our way out of our pain or read our way to healing. We are formed, not informed. We need love and relationships. As born relators and connectors, we cannot heal in isolation. Jim Wilder says this:

> The brain is more deeply changed by whom it loves (who brings me joy) than by what it thinks. Perhaps this is the real reason we have not seen the connection between spiritual formation and brain science. Too often we forget that the deepest brain change comes from our loves and not our thoughts. I am not suggesting that we abandon right thinking, much less right vision or intention, but rather that we consider adding joy to the vision, intention, and means.

When we recognize that relational love is the primary hunger of all people, we can see the pathway to healing from the devastating impacts of shame. Our souls are made for giving and receiving love. The pain of loneliness is addressed through relationships. We don't need thousands of people in our lives, but we need to do whatever it takes to bring healthy people into our lives and work to keep our relationships strong. It won't work for me to say to a client, "You are not broken. Stop thinking you are broken."

Instead, I invite them to experience my tears as I grieve their story with them. I encourage them to find people in their life who enjoy them and can accept them as they are. I invite them to have real-life experiences of joy and love.

Chris's mom died after being in a tragic, single-car accident in 2015. She survived the wreck but stayed in a coma for another ten days. This gave us time to make it to Colorado to be with her and say our final goodbyes. Both of my parents are still living, so this was my first experience of losing someone I deeply loved. She was like a second mother to me, demonstrating a tender, nurturing side of motherhood I lacked. She loved me and our children beautifully. She would always say, "Christine, your children are so happy because there is so much love in your home."

At her bedside, we said our goodbyes. We sang and prayed, held her hand and wiped her forehead. She was holding on for some reason. The nurse suggested she might not want to die in front of us, suggesting Mom could be waiting for us to leave. Although heartbroken by this, it made perfect sense. Despite raising three rowdy boys in a one-bathroom house, Chris was always amazed at how discreet she was. Modest to the very end.

It was late when we left the hospital. Her room was at the farthest end of the critical care unit, requiring us to walk the full length of the hall as we exited. The staff all knew why we were leaving. As we slowly made our way down the hall, every doctor and nurse stopped what they were doing. They reached their hands out to us, or looked up from their computers, with caring faces, mouthing, "I'm so sorry." Some even stood up to give us hugs.

We made it to the first floor, heading out to the parking lot. Just as we were about to walk out of the sliding doors, I looked up. I could not believe what I saw.

An older woman walked in, her right arm protectively around the shoulder of a younger, visibly pregnant woman, who appeared to be going into labor. I can't say for sure, but it looked very much like a mother and daughter, the mother carefully escorting her daughter to the hospital to deliver a baby.

We walked out of the doors the same moment they walked in. A mom helping her daughter have a baby. We were leaving, they were entering. We were saying goodbye, they were saying hello. Our hearts held sadness, theirs held joy.

What are the chances that we crossed the threshold to leave at the *exact* moment they entered? God allowed us to be a part of a perfectly timed, sacred encounter.

Why?

I believe he wanted me to experience a real-life depiction of the truest thing in life: From the beginning to the end, love sustains us. Love is the greatest weapon in our arsenal for fighting shame. Has love eradicated shame in my life? Of course not. But love is a necessary tool to remind ourselves of our lovability when shame shows up. Letting ourselves be known and vulnerable opens the door to love.

> # Love is the greatest weapon in our arsenal for fighting shame.

The nurse was right about Mom. We got a call that she passed before we even made it to the car. She had been waiting. And it allowed us to walk through those sliding doors when we did. And do you know what I say to Madison and Garrett when we are at their house with Nora and Ivey? *Your children are so happy because there is so much love in your home.* She loved me into a new way of loving.

When you are feeling alone, revisit a memory of someone who has shown you care and love. Our memory is stored with emotions. It is often used to bring up only painful memories. Switch it! Practice bringing up feelings of being loved and cared for. Rehearse those memories.

Use them to fight the isolation. God implores us to be *rememberers*.[11] I suppose he knows how it works since he is the one who created us to have embodied memories, rich with emotion.

> ## God implores us to be *rememberers*.

Reaching *up* is the way to access the only sustainable source of unconditional love. You are completely loved by God as you are in this current moment. When you practice receiving God's love in embodied ways, you will feel the change in your body and emotional world. Pray and envision Jesus sitting with you. Go swing and imagine Jesus laughing with you as your feet point high into the air. Sit by a lake and ask God to whisper what he thinks of you. You will begin to see who you are—your true identity. And you will come to understand that you are *never* alone.

As we close out our work on shame, I am reminded of something funny Chris and I saw when we were at the Grand Canyon. The canyon is a marvelous sight to behold; the human eye can barely fathom the majesty of it. Yet, at every turn, we saw groups of park visitors crowded around and taking pictures of squirrels!

Squirrels!

In our backyard, we have squirrels *everywhere*. I mean everywhere. We can't find a way to hang a bird feeder to keep the squirrels from dangling, twirling, and stealing the bird seed.

Since national parks draw visitors from around the world, there are people who obviously have not seen many squirrels. Swarms of visitors with cameras, phones, and selfie sticks, all amazed at the squirrel sightings. The bushy-tailed creatures are novel to them. Since squirrels are familiar to us, we ignore the silly things and keep right on hiking.

After all this talk of shame, I hope you can do what Chris and I did when we saw squirrels.

---

11 Deuteronomy 4: 9–12

Since shame is everywhere and you know how to handle it, you can see it and keep right on hiking.

I know I have talked about how dangerous shame is and its dark origins, so I sincerely hope this doesn't sound like I'm trivializing it now. But as I thought about those squirrels, I've been hoping our shame work has made you aware of it, normalized it, and given you strategies. The more you use the strategies and practice walking in healthier ways, the easier it will be to overcome shame. Notice shame, just as Chris and I glanced at the squirrels at the Grand Canyon, and then continue on your way.

Shame needs our attention. But it doesn't need all our attention.

We faced that nasty, unwanted passenger, didn't we? Shame is a tough one. Soul adventuring is about living lives of bravery and joy, which means we *must* develop the resilience to fight the one who wants to rob us of both. Shame roadblocks are not dead ends; they are passageways to bring in a more robust and resilient way of feeling and thinking into your body.

You've got this! I believe in you! You, my friend, *can* break free and move ahead in a new and beautiful way. The path before you is wide open. Let's set your route for *freedom*.

Do the Work

Love shatters shame. Name someone to whom you can reach out and spend time with this week. Talk to them about a rut or road-block you are noticing.

Do the Joy

Take fifteen minutes. Put on gentle music or nature sounds and tell yourself five different Freedom Stories from the Appendix. Allow them to linger. Take deep breaths while the feelings move throughout your body.

PART 4

Map to New Freedom

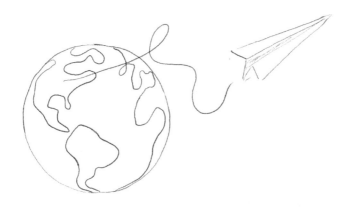

You Are a Brave Soul

FORMING BRAVE
SOUL HABITS

Long-term consistency beats short-term intensity.

——— BRUCE LEE ———

Machu Picchu, perched high in the Andes Mountains and home to awe-inspiring Inca ruins, has been on my bucket list for years. I have spent years reading about hiking through the breathtaking mountain views, exploring the sacred temples, and experiencing the enchanting town of Cusco. The time has finally come to check it off. We've booked our plane tickets and hired a guide for the Inca Trail hike!

Researching travel is all well and good but clicking the purchase button separates dreaming from doing.

It would be useless to spend hours creating the perfect itinerary for the perfect destination but never book the ticket. Never get on the plane. Is it fun and interesting to plan a trip? Sure. But planning alone won't get you the memories of being on that beach or strolling the streets in that romantic village or jumping in victory on the top of a mountain. Getting information about travel is altogether different from traveling.

We are inundated with information on social media, blogs, news channels, and podcasts. To be clear, information is a good thing. But if all we do is read and click, click and read, screenshot and save, change is unlikely.

Reading and learning new information is, of course, a wonderful thing! I'm inviting you to read and gather more information right now. But simply *consuming* information will not get you where you want to go.

To go further on your soul adventure, action is required. Why? Because what is not practiced is not understood.

> # What is not practiced
> # is not understood.

Your soul needs *more* than information. James K. A. Smith notes, "For our spiritual hungers, new knowledge and information might help me see the power of bad habits, but that is not sufficient to undo them. I can't 'know' my way to new habits."

Doing brings learning. Doing creates new habits.

Now that we have developed shame resilience and know how to get out of ruts and move past roadblocks, the next part of our adventure involves putting these new habits into practice. Brave Soul Habits strengthen your shame resilience and empower you to live your big, bold, joy-filled life. It is one of the most powerful ways to fight shame.

The good news is your brain is built with the capacity to change and form new habits. It may take a while. Heck, it may take a lifetime. But every positive action is a step forward.

Brave Soul Habit #1: Gather

This is the power of gathering: it inspires us,
delightfully, to be more hopeful, more joyful,
more thoughtful: in a word, more alive.

———————————————— ALICE WATERS ————————————————

We are built to love up close.

The internet will spoon feed us stories of a crumbling, divided world. It will tell us of all the things to fear, the people to hate, the groups to stand against.

Listen, I'm no Pollyanna. I know there are hard, awful realities in our world. But things are not as bad as the internet would lead us to believe. The internet *needs* us to stay outraged so we'll keep clicking. And clicking. And clicking.

What if we didn't? What if we did something else—something more powerful than an internet rant ever could be?

Gather.

Instead of clicking, gather.

Instead of complaining, gather.

Instead of scrolling on your lunch break, gather.

Even if it's not your turn to send the invite, gather.

When we gather with people in relational spaces, we experience the opposite of hate and division. We experience connection. Joy. Bonding. Kindness.

Gathering is a skill I learned from my parents. They are gatherers. Our home was a whirlwind of activity for large family gatherings, like a rural, less crowded version of Grand Central Station. And with cows. The men would assemble under one of the giant oak trees where Dad did all his barbequing. They sat in a hodgepodge collection of woven lawn chairs, shooting the breeze while tending to the fire.

The kitchen was always buzzing with hurried activity. My mom and aunts moved around each other with a knowing grace, their steps seemingly choreographed to a familiar tune only the four of them could hear. They chatted while setting out the mashed potatoes, peeling the saran wrap off the deviled eggs, stirring up the sweet tea—with two full cups of sugar, thank you very much. The kids were off running around, staying out of the way of the adults. There was a cadence to it, a familiar rhythm I can feel in my bones.

When we gather, hope is alive. Love abounds.

Choose to build relational spaces instead of being sucked into the current climate of sorting people into categories of who is against us or who is with us. One fills us with life, the other drains us of it.

In January 2023, as I began *again* on this book, I gathered six dear friends for a weekend together at a lake house. They were all from different stages in my adult life. I had been purposefully working to face my self-sufficiency and Lone Ranger tendencies (avoidant attachment at work). I intentionally asked the people in my life for help and encouragement in real time: my writing posse. I needed them, and I told them those exact words.

This was me practicing the Brave Soul Habit of gathering my people.

One flew in from North Carolina, three drove in from the Dallas area, one from Houston, and one from Huntsville. I amassed all their favorite foods and cocktails. We had two fantastic days together. We encouraged each other, belly laughed, and watched the sunset over the lake. I specifically asked them to pray for me. I invited them to help me see my blind spots, asking them to speak into the areas I might not be able to see for myself. It was the perfect send-off for me to write my book.

These friends have been encouraging to me every step of the way. I have texted them on big writing days, told them when I've been stuck. Each of them has reached out during this extended writing season. I'm grateful to be loved so lavishly. I also reached out to numerous other friends along the way, being honest about my desire to get it done and letting them know when I felt stuck. As I neared the end, I sent them a text: "This is the last time I'm asking for prayers! I'm almost to the finish line!" My phone blew up with words of encouragement, hearts, memes, smiley faces, and party poppers.

You will not regret the work of building relationships. Shame disintegrates and destroys relationships. Love is a habit. Build it. Practice it. Practice letting people in, letting them love you, letting them see you when you are not okay. Be a giver *and* a receiver. It's a value we must hold near and dear. Remember, we are loved into new ways of loving.

Invite someone to coffee. Send the first text. Walk up to a friend you haven't talked to in a while. A little effort will go a long way. My writing posse is excitedly awaiting our reunion weekend at the lake house. We're going to gather to celebrate, to laugh, to give some high fives, and dream of what God has in store for us next.

Depending on your personality, you may gather one or two. We don't need a giant number. You + one = a gathering.

You can't wait for relationships to come to you. Keep practicing relationships. Keep practicing gathering.

Brave Soul Habit #2: Drop the Rope

We are dying from overthinking. We are slowly
killing ourselves by thinking about everything.
Think. Think. Think.

ANTHONY HOPKINS

Let's do some imagining together. I want to show you how overthinking works.

Imagine you are holding a giant rope with a large white ribbon tied in a bow where your hands grip the rope. The rope goes on as far as you can see to both your left and your right. It reaches to infinity.

The white ribbon represents this present moment. The left side of the ribbon represents the future. The right side, the past.

Imagine that you begin to worry about something. The voice of anxiety always uses the words, *"What if?"* As you worry about the issue, asking the *what if* question, you let go of that spot where the ribbon is tied and grab the rope to your left, into the future. You take a step to the left as you envision the *what if,* your hands moving along the rope. As you engage the next *what if* scenario in your mind, you take more steps to the left. The longer you envision another *what if,* the farther you go to the left, the farther you go into the future.

Following the *what if* questions is overthinking into the future. Your brain is a time traveler. When it travels through time, emotions and anxiety travel along.

Now imagine you are way down the rope in the future, and you look back to see the white ribbon. Your nervous system, your emotions are in the future, but all the resources you need to handle this current moment are back at the white ribbon, in the present moment.

The same holds true when ruminating about the past, which is also overthinking, only in the other direction.

Let's imagine you're ruminating on something you said in a conversation with your boss, something you regret. As you enter the memory and say things like, "Why did I say that? I always say stupid stuff. I should have said _____ instead." You were holding the white ribbon before you began ruminating; now you are walking to your right. Regret and shame pulling you into the past, overthinking what you should have done. Every ruminating thought of *I should have* or *Why didn't I?* takes you further down the rope to the right. Remember, the rope is infinite in length. The longer you think through the regret, the further you move to the right, activating more emotions.

Now imagine looking back and seeing the white ribbon. Your nervous system, your emotions are in the past, but all the resources you need to handle this current moment are back at the white ribbon, in the present moment.

The further you follow the rope in either direction into overthinking, the more anxiety your body will feel. What is the answer to this dreadful dilemma?

Drop the Rope.

No matter which way you tend to travel, the Brave Soul Habit you need to quell the anxious storm is to Drop the Rope.

Once you've dropped the rope, see yourself standing with the white ribbon at your feet, marking this present moment. Your back is straight, your shoulders are strong. You and the ribbon are in the center of your hula hoop. Healthy soul work allows you to contemplate your future and our past, but you are doing it from a place of calm groundedness.

In the present moment . . .

- You have all you need for life and godliness. (2 Peter 1:3)
- You have immeasurably more than you can ask or imagine. (Ephesians 3:20)
- You have all you need for today, like the flowers and the birds. (Matthew 6:25–36)
- You have been given grace upon grace. (John 1:16)

With the rope at your feet, you have access to your prefrontal cortex, which helps you problem-solve, connect to God and others, regulate emotions, make informed choices. Overthinking will never produce healthy results. You may come up with answers, but your energy resources will be drained, leaving you exhausted and stressed.

With the white ribbon at your feet, take a few cleansing breaths, telling yourself you have everything you need to handle the anxieties and regrets of life. In this spot, you have the ability to manage yourself and your life. Your forgiveness processes are there at the white ribbon. Your tools to manage your ruts and roadblocks are easily accessible. If your *what ifs* involve someone else, remind yourself you cannot control what is in their hula hoop. If you are regretting something you said, remind yourself you cannot control other people's response to you. Remind yourself when you learn better, you do better.

This is the perfect time to pick up some manna. The white ribbon reminds you to gather all you need in this moment *for* this moment. When you drop the rope, you are unencumbered by the past or the future and free to reach out and pick up what you need.

- Call or text a friend to talk through the situation.
- Talk to God about your anxiety or your regret. He is an ever-present help in time of need. (Psalm 46:1)
- Take a walk while deep breathing and repeat to yourself, "I have everything I need."
- Journal about the situation.
- Remind yourself you can contemplate the problem from a healthier space at a later time.

Tell that time-traveling brain of yours to Drop the Rope. Your life is unfolding in the present moment. Be here for it.

Brave Soul Habit #3: Rest and Slowing

Hurry is the great enemy of souls in our day. There is no way a soul can thrive when it is hurried. We must ruthlessly eliminate hurry from our lives.

— DALLAS WILLARD —

It is cause for great alarm around our house if I'm out of creamer. I'm one of those coffee drinkers who sips their coffee on the golden side of brown. I know, I know. The *real* coffee drinkers out there are rolling their eyes at me. You can try all you want to convince me of the sophistication of that pure black stuff with those rich flavors. *Blah, blah, blah.* Save it for someone else. My generous pour of vanilla cream is the very reason I get out of bed.

Back to being out of creamer. After our morning workout, Chris and I stopped by H-E-B so I could grab some. I hopped out of the car and headed straight to the dairy section. An older man grinned at me and said, "Woah there. You're in quite a hurry! Whatcha in such a hurry for?" I looked at him awkwardly, unsure why he said that. As I checked in with my surroundings, I realized I had been running, literally running, down the aisle.

It was 7:00 a.m. The store was virtually empty. I had no appointments until 10:00 a.m. There was absolutely no reason to be running. It is as if urgency is a part of my personality. I tend to hurry through life. I want more of everything, and I want it quickly. Do you even want to know how many speeding tickets I've gotten in my life? I think not.

You may not be quite as *Energizer-bunny-ish* as I, but the truth is we are an urgent, anxious, busy, distracted generation of people. The pace of life, the pressure to perform, the pull of getting it all done can keep us in a never-ending battle against time.

However.

Our souls are built for spaciousness, for rest. Our souls need time to ponder and think. Our brave lives can only be lived when they are allowed the opportunity to be restored and renewed through listening to the wisdom of God, bringing us back to the sufficiency of the current moment. Parker Palmer, author of *Let Your Life Speak,* offers this beautiful metaphor:

> The soul is like a wild animal—tough, resilient, savvy, self-sufficient and yet exceedingly shy. If we want to see a wild animal, the last thing we should do is to go crashing through the woods, shouting for the creature to come out. But if we are willing to walk quietly into the woods and sit silently for an hour or two at the base of a tree, the creature we are waiting for may well emerge, and out of the corner of an eye we will catch a glimpse of the precious wildness we seek.

Rest is a sacred gateway to knowing the deep workings of our souls. Most of us, however, live loud, chaotic, noisy lives that chase away the opportunity to hear the voice of our soul. Often defined by our jobs and busyness, we are working more and sleeping less, making us sicker. Insufficient sleep has been correlated with a rise of chronic diseases and conditions. When we enter rest, we are practicing the spiritual discipline of release: release of our need to produce, our addiction to control, our obsession with performance.

Rest is a sacred gateway to knowing the deep workings of our souls.

And, oh, how God delights in us as we rest! Sabbath is God's grand idea, an invitation to release our attachment to work. We are made to be transformed by beauty, the taste of a good meal, silence, connected relationships, the feeling of sand in our toes, bright sunsets, heart-forward conversations, a child's giggles.

The limitless access we have to mind-numbing digital content only makes rest more challenging to find. Technology has invaded every single part of our lives, making our fast lives move even faster. We multitask, scroll at red lights, tell Alexa our grocery lists.

Our creativity will shrivel under such pressure to go, do, and constantly consume. Our relationships will suffer, dried up by the drought of care and nurture they need.

Ruthlessly fight the world's invitation to stay busy and distracted. We must *rest*. We must *slow*.

Rest is to be a friend, a habit. A rhythm. A way of life. Listen to this sacred invitation to rest and slowing:

> "Are you tired? Worn out? Burned out on religion? Come to me. Get away with me and you'll recover your life. I'll show you how to take a real rest. Walk with me and work with me—watch how I do it. Learn the unforced rhythms of grace. I won't lay anything heavy or ill-fitting on you. Keep company with me and you'll learn to live freely and lightly."
>
> —Matthew 11:28–30, TM

We must be brave enough to enter and embrace rest and slowing.

We must be brave enough to enter and embrace rest and slowing. It is not easy. But it is worth it.

Shhhhh . . . listen. I hear it.

That wild, beautiful soul of yours is waiting to emerge.

Brave Soul Habit #4: Hire a New Manager

Compassion for others begins
with kindness to ourselves.

PEMA CHODRON

This brave soul habit is fun: time to fire some bad management.

Here's a scenario of James, an employee in a clothing store. Let's say I throw some fairy dust into the store, creating magic to help us with an experiment. James works a day with one manager and relives the exact same day with a different manager. His performance is the same under both managers.

Monday, Manager #1

The first manager walks up to James, seething with frustration. In an irritated voice she yells, "What is wrong with you? Could you please tell me why you act like this job is so hard? I've told you over and over and over, do not fold the clothes in the back! Do you ever even listen? You are such an idiot. On top of that, you never fold the shirts *correctly*."

She wasn't done yet, "You may be getting a little over minimum wage, but you are not worth what we pay you. You are lucky I even decided to give you a chance, but I'm doubting that decision more every day."

Disgusted, the manager rolls her eyes. "I've had lazy workers before, but you are one of the worst I've seen." She raises her eyebrows, purses her lips, and storms away.

Monday, Manager #2

The second manager walks up to James, smiling. "Good morning! It's hard to believe this place has already been ravaged by the customers. Seems like they unfolded every shirt! You have a tough job. It's hard to keep up! I know we don't pay much here. I appreciate how you give this job everything you've got. As a reminder, let's fold those shirts in the front first, okay?"

She cheered him on. "I know the job can be mindless! It's a challenge to keep up. Thanks for caring by working your way all the way to the back. A quick reminder on the fold; be sure to make it crisp and clean so the customers can see the front of the shirt as they walk by. I really appreciate you! Thanks for your faithfulness to the task!"

Okay, the magic has worn off. Let's check in with James.

Imagine how he feels working under the direction of the first manager. How will he feel about going to work? How do you think his performance will be? How will he feel while he works? What will he be like when the manager walks up to give him feedback next time?

Let's do the same thing with the second manager. How will he feel about going to work? How do you think his performance will be? How will he feel while he works? What will he be like when the manager walks up to give him feedback next time?

Take a pause from those managers and let me tell you something about how our nervous systems operate. When an outside event (being yelled at, accused, blamed) alerts our nervous system, it becomes dysregulated. Survival brain takes over to protect self and activates anxiety.

The shocking thing is that the same thing happens to our nervous system when *our internal voice* does the yelling. When we yell at ourselves, even if we never speak the words aloud, it disrupts our emotional world and can flip our lid.

Think about that for a moment. When you are mad at yourself for a mistake or mad at your performance, it doesn't make your internal world better; it makes it worse. You are less likely to operate from your integrated brain, where you can be fully present and regulate your emotions.

Remember my "Christine Can Make Mistakes" story after my conversation with Colton? When I went on a walk, the reality hit me that, somewhere deep down, I did not believe I had the right to make a mistake. Shame had hooked me with the lie that I wasn't allowed to be human and make mistakes. When I cried out, I was reminding myself I am a work in progress.

Manager #1 constantly ran the show when I believed that yelling and fussing at myself was the best way to get myself in order. That voice told me over and over again that God was mad at me for messing up, for not moving fast enough, for forgetting to do something. For everything. Shame lied to me and said all that fussing was deserved.

Oh, by the way, *you* are the two managers. Time to fire Manger #1 and hire Manger #2.

I've been practicing this Brave Soul Habit, and I'm getting better and better at it.

When I work with clients surrounding this issue, they almost always tell me they show grace to others and not to themselves. They say they are only hard on themselves, not others. Sadly, it doesn't work that way. In her excellent book called *Self-Compassion*, Kristen Neff says, "If you are continually judging and criticizing yourself while trying to be kind to others, you are drawing artificial boundaries and distinctions that only lead to feelings of separation and isolation."

One explanation might be that our primal brain wants an enemy, looking to find who is bad and who is good. It started with the blame shifting in the Garden of Eden. *It's her fault. It's the serpent's fault. It's your fault.* It's quickest to move directly into self-blame. Manager #1 in charge and wreaking havoc.

Practice using our slowing tools. Is the voice you hear a friend or a foe? Embody a kinder, gentler voice. Learn to listen for that voice, especially when you make a mistake or when you are in pain. Practice talking to yourself the way you would talk to a good friend when they are in hurting. Allow yourself to be human. To make mistakes.

Fire that bad boy and get you a kinder manager, okay?

Brave Soul Habit #5: Embracing Grief and Lament

I have woven a parachute out of everything broken.

———— WILLIAM STAFFORD ————

I was so, so sad.

The moving trucks were long gone, the kitchen unpacked. We were well on our way to establishing our new life in Huntsville. I told you about Chris's job loss. It was hard. Moving seemed even harder. It was only fifty-two miles down the road, but I felt a thousand miles from the life I left. I wanted to rewind the clock, return to an earlier mark on my timeline. I didn't want to live in Huntsville. It was like wearing stiff, heavy denim when all I wanted was soft, comfy pajamas.

People were kind and gracious to us. Everything looked fine on the outside, yet inside, I was secretly hemorrhaging sadness. And defiance.

Our old life was in the rearview mirror. The month I graduated from graduate school with my counseling degree was the same month we moved. I was starting over in every way possible. New church, new home, new friends, new career.

Also new wounds, new grief, new cynicism, new doubts, new pain.

I had a friend tell me, "Christine, it's okay to get fetal. Curl up on the couch and let yourself grieve." That is exactly what I did. I made space in my soul to feel my losses and name my sadness.

Most of us think grief is only for funerals. Even then, many place a high value on people who hold it together during their grief. We are a *"I'm fine. I'm fine. I have to be strong,"* kind of culture. Many tell me they don't want to play the victim card, or they wrongly believe their loss is not as bad as someone else's pain. Grief is not comparative. Remember those beach balls and pressure cookers? Grief is not intended to be buried.

Entering grief is not about glorifying our pain or wearing our suffering as a badge of honor. It's not about seeing who has it worse or minimizing our hurts. It's about telling the truth, telling the truth of living in a broken world, where we experience loss, betrayal, disappointments, and shattered dreams.

Thankfully, God made a way for us to process our pain. Jesus proclaimed a counterculture means to happiness, flipping conventional wisdom upside down. He offers these words to us, "Blessed are those who mourn, for they will be comforted" (Matthew 5:4, NIV).

Jesus doesn't just give us permission to grieve, but he identifies grief as a path to joy. We cannot selectively repress emotion. When we push down the sorrow, we push down the joy. Opening our soul to grief is opening our soul to all the beauty as well.

I love how Miriam Greenspan calls the grief-to-joy process *alchemy*:

> Finding the power of the sacred, not despite suffering, but in the midst of it: This is the alchemy of dark emotions. Through this alchemy, grief moves us from sorrow for what we've lost to gratitude for what remains. Fear of life's fragility is transformed to the joy of living fully, with openness. And even despair becomes the ground of resilient faith—not just an opiate for our pain, but a profound commitment to life as it is.

In neurological terms, pain is pain. The same neurons fire when you have physical pain as when we are in emotional pain. When we have a physical injury, we attend to it. We are to do the same with our emotional injuries.

My little granddaughter Nora fell out of the swing at our house, landing face first. My heart lurched when I saw her hit the ground. I ran across the yard and swooped her up. Holding her in my arms, I looked for the injury. As she cried, I acknowledged how scared she must've been and how much it must have hurt. I held her until she was ready to do something else.

Our souls need the same kind of care when we experience emotional pain.

Grief allows our souls to release what it once had, making room for what is next. It is the natural rhythm of releasing, lamenting, and accepting the new reality.

We do not have to be strong. We hurt when we lose things, and grief points to the truth of what we have lost. We can grieve over all sorts of things:

- the change of a life season
- a dream that never materialized
- a job loss
- a child growing up
- a relationship shift
- an aging parent
- a disappointing job change

Grief needs to be broken down into bite-sized pieces and named specifically. One event/situation can have multiple losses. Zoom in as much as possible on the specifics of the small losses in the situation. We cannot forgive what we have not grieved. If we want to forgive, we first grieve what we lost. To grieve, we must tell the truth. Both require the gentle presence of Christ.

> ## We cannot forgive what we have not grieved.

Did you know the tears we cry when we hurt emotionally have a different chemistry than the tears that well up in our eyes when we cut an onion? Tears of pain are thicker, causing them to stream more slowly. It's as if they are made to be seen. They are crafted to sit on the cheeks longer so someone can witness them, see them—see *us*—and offer comfort.

Entering grief and lament is a Brave Soul Habit. It is a gift to your soul.

Brave Soul Habit #6: Practice Delight

We must risk delight. We must have the stubbornness to accept our gladness in the ruthless furnace of this world.

———————— JACK GILBERT ————————

You've heard about a lot of my weaknesses while we have been soul adventuring. I've done my best to be honest about my struggles.

But let me tell you what, this Brave Soul Habit, *delight*, is my specialty. Delight shows up in so many ways, but I want to share just three.

Delight in Play

If you go back to look at the ruts, you will notice they are almost exclusively about *pressure and performance*, whether it is pressure to please, to be in control, to be perfect. Except for one. One rut is a feeble attempt to cope with all those never-ending pressures.

Numbing.

Managing life's pressures by numbing is as useless as holding a finger on a dam's leak. One of the sincerest invitations I pose to those struggling with alcohol abuse is, "You are drinking, but let's explore what you are really thirsty for." Numbing pretends to give relief, but it lies. An analgesic ointment will soothe the ulcer pain in your mouth, but if you use it every day, you lose the exquisite gift of taste. Deadening yourself to life will block you from experiencing the joy you desperately desire.

So, what is an answer to this dark dilemma?

Play. Delight in play.

Years ago, I was introduced to a YouTube video by Dr. Stuart Brown, a psychiatrist and founder of the National Institute for Play. In the video, Brown walks the audience through an incident randomly captured by an artic photographer. It was a rare encounter of a polar bear playing with an arctic wolf. The encounter began when the artic wolf, which could easily be breakfast for the bear, put his front paws down in front of the bear in what is called a canine's play bow. Essentially, the prey invited the predator to play. And he did. They romped and rolled in the snow for no reason at all. Other than the joy of playing.

We need more of what those two creatures were doing. Playing, for no reason whatsoever. Being friends instead of enemies. Creating a free, open space where our souls can be light, unencumbered by the heaviness of life. If we work and numb, and then work and numb, rinse and repeat, we are trapped. We will be stuck in a never-ending cycle of performing for our worthiness, crashing, then using an analgesic for the pain.

Back to our brain science. We cannot play when our threat system is activated. Survival mode and play mode are opposite functions in the brain. You know by now which one is the front and which one is back. Play is vital to healthy and whole lives.

God built us to play. It is a Brave Soul Habit. We are formed by delight, and we are sustained by delight. Play is our way to bravely fight against the heaviness of our world.

Play doesn't happen by accident, though. It is a habit you must pursue. In his insightful book *Play: How it Shapes the Brain, Opens the Imagination, and Invigorates the Soul*, Stuart Brown says, "The opposite of play is not work; the opposite of play is depression." He interviewed males incarcerated for homicide and found major play deficits in their life histories. My point is not that you could become homicidal if you don't play. It's simply to recognize that we are at risk of serious life dysfunctions without the life-giving benefits of play. He goes on to say "Play is the stick that stirs the drink. It is the basis of all art, games, books, sports, movies, fashion, fun, and wonder—in short, the basis of what we think of as civilization. Play is the vital essence of life. It is what makes life lively."

Play is countercultural to the world of production. We must fight against that. I have developed a habit of asking someone I meet for the first time, *What do you love?* instead of *What do you do?* They usually stumble around awkwardly at first. We are conditioned to identify ourselves by what we do. We will not produce anything when we play. We are inviting our souls to be light and free.

My dad had a knack for fun. He would always smile and tell us how much his grandpa taught him how to be playful. We didn't play board games; we invented our own games, usually involving balls of all shapes and sizes—bouncy balls, footballs, basketballs, the works. We would bounce, throw, or kick the balls. The rules were fluid, constantly evolving to keep the game exciting and silly. If the rules didn't work, we would make new ones.

Why? For no other reason than joy. My dad is a hard-working man. It was a gift to see him break away from work to play silly, made-up games with us. This unplanned, unrehearsed play established a lighthearted way in my soul.

Chris and I made an intentional effort for play to be central in our home. We had all-family trampoline jump nights. We would surprise the kids after bedtime, kidnapping them out of their beds to get ice cream in their pajamas. The play continues to this day. At our last family beach vacation, the girls schemed and ordered new matching swimsuits for the guys. They just so happened to be suits that disintegrated when they got wet. Yes. They completely fell apart. I have evidence. The pics are on the Soul Adventuring Scenes. Don't worry, they are PG.

Play is a free, open space where our souls can be light and free, unencumbered by the heaviness of life.

In other words, our soul adventures need play to make them happen.

Delight in Nature

Nature Deficit Disorder is a term that acknowledges that humans are spending less time outdoors. Closed in manmade spaces. Wired to screens. Disconnected from nature and one another.

This deficit can lead to all sorts of issues. Children and adults alike, reduced to living small lives with big problems.

Entering our big, beautiful world can help us live bigger lives with smaller problems.

Nature sits waiting. Inviting. Beckoning. Say yes.

Please. You will be better for it. With all the hard work you have been doing, you must get outside to make your growth efforts sustainable.

- Put your feet on the grass.
- Watch the sky.
- Listen to the birds.
- Work through your emotions on a walk in your neighborhood.
- Practice your boundary language aloud in your backyard.
- Tell your story to a friend while sitting at a park.
- When your lid flips and you can't get outside, tell Alexa or Siri to play nature sounds.

The primary way I knew I wanted to write was realizing how beautifully I wrote when I was outside. Sitting at campfires, looking over cliff edges, driving across mountain passes, words coursed through my soul. I wrote much of this book while on camping trips, overseas adventures, and at our giant farm table that is centered in the middle of our forested backyard haven.

I'm a firm believer that God built us to have sacred encounters with nature. The encounters are unique to each person, each moment. The wind refuses to be cliché. It exhales to bend the branches in a slightly new way for each passing witness. Every nanosecond of every day, a different molecule of water collides on the rocks as it cascades down, choreographing a unique river dance with each passing moment. God has given flowers the autonomy to careen their neck in any direction they can find life-giving sunlight. Nature delights us by being wild and charming, untamed and inviting, ancient and fresh, colorful and fierce. God gave us the gift of our senses, the capacity to notice these small, ever-changing miracles. He created us with souls that are stirred by these miraculous displays.

We get out of our heads by getting into our body, and nothing in the world brings us into our bodies like the beauty and tranquility of nature. God allowed beauty to open our eyes to new truths about him and about ourselves. We can feel his love in profound ways when we delight in nature. I'm not sure how looking at mountains and rivers, trees and birds can do that, but God has made a way for it.

> We get out of our heads by getting into our body, and nothing in the world brings us into our bodies like the beauty and tranquility of nature.

You don't have to be in Yosemite, Yellowstone, Uganda, or Utah. You simply need to slow down and look up. Breathe in and breathe out. Look around and glance within.

Nature is waiting to bring you into delight.

Spiritual Delight

In the past, I have often experienced God as someone who was frustrated with me. Since learning about the effects of trauma on our development, as well as the healing power of delighted attachment, I've been practicing new ways of interacting with God. This is our final Brave Soul Habit: the habit of spiritual delight.

The practice of spiritual delight is about developing a practice of experiencing God as looking at you and toward you with delight and joy. Even though we have already talked about delight in nature, I believe these two practices go hand in hand, beautifully weaving a tapestry of relational connectedness to self and God.

On our 8,000-mile national park road trip, we saw beauty almost beyond measure. It was more than scenery. It was personal. It was as if God was orchestrating encounters with nature that were uniquely beautiful to me and uniquely delightful to my soul.

We were on a hike to a waterfall in Sequoia National Park. As we were on our way, a man was on his way back from the falls. He stopped us as we were climbing, looked directly at me, and said, "Wow. I'm from this area, and I've never seen the falls this beautiful." Another time, at the Golden Gate bridge, a man was taking our picture. After handing the phone back to me, he said, "Wow. What a day you got today! I'm a local, and it is almost always foggy this time of year and this time of day." It was as if their comments were intentionally directed at me.

We were on a Jenny Lake hike in the Grand Tetons, pondering a decision, a deep philosophical dilemma. I was in turmoil as I considered my options. Chris and I were tossing pros and cons around about the situation as we hiked. I felt at an impasse, the conclusion out of reach.

For some reason, I began to reflect on all the small, delightful encounters I'd had on this trip. Encounters that seemed to be specially made for me, instances of pure delight orchestrated by God. I looked up at a brilliant display of beauty, and it hit me.

God is not stuck in my dilemma! He is not caught in my either/or. He is not confused. If I live in his love and in his delight, I am free from this dilemma because he is free! He is not bound. I am not bound.

This insight did not give me specific, immediate answers, but it took away my fear of getting it wrong. God's freedom set me free to live in delight and wonder. I felt seen and overwhelmed by his goodness toward me.

In that moment, it was as if my emotional bucket had dipped down into the infinite well of God's love and been filled anew. His well never runs dry. No one who cranks down their bucket into this well will come up empty. No one. And one small splash of that water can set us alive and make us free.

Those types of sacred encounters have inspired me to incorporate this Brave Soul habit into my daily life. When I am in a hard spot in a session with a client, I glance in my mind's eye toward a loving Father who delights in my desire to help people walk in freedom. When I'm playing dominoes with my aging parents, and I begin to feel the fear of losing them, I see God with me, assuring he is proud of me for showing up to be with them today, in this moment.

Spiritual delight comes from seeing God see you. Watching him enjoy you, be proud of you. The story of Hagar is found in Genesis 16. I won't tell her whole story, but life handed her some tough stuff. She was having a hard time. She had been rejected and cast out of her community. Abandoned and alone. And God showed up for her. He not only showed up, he *saw* her—truly saw her. She is the only person in Scripture to give God a name. She named God *The God Who Sees*. Or more accurately, the *God of Seeing*.

> ## Spiritual delight comes from seeing God see you.

We often think of God seeing us when we have done wrong. Practicing spiritual delight means allowing yourself to be seen by our always-available God, who is delighted in you, full of love for you. He is available to see you and soothe you, providing the secure attachment your soul most needs.

PART 5

Adventure Awaits

Onward to Living with Bravery and Joy

THE ADVENTURE AHEAD

If you want to build a ship, don't drum up
people to collect wood and don't assign them
tasks and work, but rather teach them to long
for the endless immensity of the sea.

— ANTOINE DE SAINT-EXUPÉRY —

After our son Landon moved into his new apartment in down-town Houston, we were chatting about what he loves and doesn't love about it. He enjoys the cool vibe of urban liv-ing. He doesn't like driving past two dumpsters outside his apartment building on his way home every day. They are large, always full, and stinky. It makes coming home feel less inviting.

He went on to describe the nostalgia he feels when coming to our home, especially for Christmas. When our kids were in college, we made sure all the outside lights and garland were up by the time they came home for Christmas. We wanted them to drive down our street, and as they neared the house, to see and feel Christmas before they even walked in the door. Landon's memory of coming home for Christmas is why driving by the dumpsters at his new apartment has taken some adjustments. It's because he likes *the feeling of coming home.*

Our time together is nearing its completion, and we are heading home. But where is home? What's next? I mentioned earlier how C.S. Lewis frequently wrote about the longings deep within each of us. I have always found this concept so beautiful: longing for somewhere we have never been, something we have never heard, yet longing for it as if we know it. In *Mere Christianity* he said, "If we find ourselves with a desire that nothing in this world can satisfy, the most probable explanation is that we were made for another world."

My hope is that you will continue to follow the longing Lewis wrote about, adventuring and exploring the rest of your lives for the place of ultimate joy: God himself.

Only now you have a few more pieces of essential gear than you had before. A few more skills. And hopefully a lot more insight into who you are.

Soul adventures do not end like fairytales, *happily ever after.* New adventures await! Do you remember the Choose Your Own Adventure books? Unlike traditional stories, the book series allows you to make your own choices at key points in the story, encouraging you to be an active participant in the unfolding of the story. Soul adventuring is a lot like those books. There is more than one way forward. You have choices every single day. You get to decide which dreams to pursue and what mountains to climb.

Only now you are equipped with the tools and strategies to navigate whatever adventures you choose to take. I'm confident you are more aware of that unwanted passenger who will most certainly attempt to sabotage your bravery and joy. And with your shame-resilience skills, I'm also confident you can overcome whatever resistance you face.

The Messy Path of Growth

Brave lives make room for mistakes. Mistakes can be messy. The truth is, growth is always messy. It will be littered with mistakes. Your path to your brave life will not be one straight line.

This is often what we hope growth will look like.

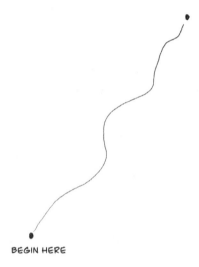

Growth looks more like this.

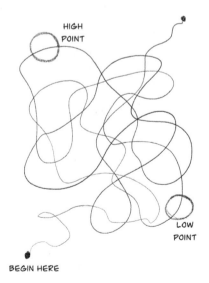

On the messy path of growth, we need to be aware of two dangers. The first is shown by the circle around the high point. This is when we are seeing big changes and wonderful transformations. When you are at that high point, be careful about thinking, "I'm done!" It feels good to grow. Enjoy it. Don't be tempted, though, to believe you will never cycle back down.

The other danger is to judge a low spot. See the circle on the bottom? When we are not doing well or when change is hard to see, we tend to get fatalistic, saying things to ourselves like, "I'll never change." When you are in a low spot, remind yourself *this is part of the messy path of growth*. Don't bring that critical internal manager back. Be gentle. Show yourself grace.

We are never truly done. We keep at it, keep working. Never stop trying, always starting again. When we get off course, we can find our way back. Paul Tournier writes in *The Strong the Weak*, "We are always turning back to that which we have turned away from." It brings me hope to accept the reality that life is messy and tangled.

It reminds me of a trail in Zion National Park. We hiked Angel's Landing in Zion in 2016. Angel's Landing is renowned for being one of the most intense hikes in the park. It boasts a staggering twenty-one switchbacks. At the turn of every one of those dreaded switchbacks, it felt like we would never, ever get to the top. That is a lot of weaving and turning to find the path up. In and out, up and back. That is the messy path of growth.

Pending

Man cannot discover new oceans unless he has
the courage to lose sight of the shore.

— ANDRÉ GIDE —

The only time I have travel anxiety is if I fear something is at risk of actually *not* happening. If we miss a hike we wanted to take. If we don't get to all the things on our itinerary.

On our last trip to New Zealand in 2023, we had a 9:50 p.m. flight out of Houston on Easter Sunday. While finishing our online flight check-in the night before, a warning screen flashed on my screen. It said we could not check in until we completed the New Zealand travel visa application. It gave us the link to download an app to begin that process. No worries. We downloaded it, filled out the required information, and paid a $52 tourist visa fee.

The next screen stated our application status: PENDING. Then, in small letters, it said, "The application takes between twenty-four and seventy-two hours to be processed."

We were leaving in twenty-three hours! With the time change, their offices would be closed the following day for the Easter Holiday.

We continued to pack, but the pit in my stomach would not subside. My gut felt like rocks tumbling in a rock polishing machine. All my trip excitement had disappeared. I tried to reassure myself there was no way this pending application would prevent us from boarding the plane. We had a twelve-day camping itinerary in a camper van across the South Island, a one-week stay with Chris's brother in the North Island, and then I was staying another week to write.

Our adventure was threatened with that one word: *pending*.

Pending. Waiting. Anticipating. Unfinished.

You know that feeling, right? It's a terrible *in-between-ness* of wanting to do something but feeling too stuck or afraid to do it.

As we near the end of our adventure, take some time to reflect: What are some of the situations in your life you feel are pending? What is keeping you from living the life you were built to live? What are some unfinished dreams, unexplored visions? Do you have projects you want to start? Relationships you want to heal? Take a few moments. Write down what might be pending. It is important to be specific. Name it.

Who knows what kinds of incredible things God has *in you* that he wants to do *through you*. I am grinning as I imagine all the brave and beautiful dreams and visions sitting in pending categories all over the world, waiting to be unleashed. I love how author Parker Palmer says it, "Every journey, honestly undertaken, stands a chance of taking us toward the place where our deep gladness meets the world's deep need." Look out, world! There are some soul adventurers getting set free and ready to do their thing.

I suppose you know we made the flight, right? We showed up at the airport to check in. The application said it was still pending, but the boarding agent winked and scanned our boarding passes. I have the same kind of hope for the pending visions God has placed on your heart.

Be Bad at New Things

My mom carries herself with a strong joy. In fact, Joy is her middle name. When it comes to trying new things, she was a force to be reckoned with. She was cheerfully determined that Michael and I would not be isolated Arneckeville country kids, lacking the necessary skills to put ourselves out into this great big world. She wasn't anything like the helicopter or snowplow parents of our day. She was more like the proverbial momma bird, nudging the **fledgling** out of the nest, forcing it to fly. She made us try things. Lots of things. I had an elaborate insect collection, labels and all, in a green hand-built wooden box. (My brother made the box. Maybe that's when I should have started building boxes!) I learned to play piano, sew, crochet, and macramé. I competed at the state level in 4-H public speaking competitions—as a *twelve*-year-old! I had leadership roles in every kind of organization. Her gentle prodding continues to this very day as she regularly checks in about the book, the one she was confident I could write.

Cultivating a life of bravery and joy goes beyond healing and mending. It's also about taking the risk to try new things.

Experiment with a new thing. And remember that mistakes are part of the adventure. It's okay to be bad at your new stuff! God built us to grow, repair, learn, investigate, practice, explore.

> ## Experiment with a new thing.
> ## And remember that mistakes
> ## are part of the adventure.

So, try new things!

Be bad at them until you get good at them.

I know. It's uncomfortable. No one likes discomfort, but growth and discomfort are intricately connected.

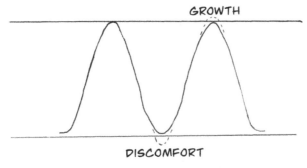

This is what I call the growth wave. The top line is growth; the bottom line is discomfort. We all want the growth to pop through the top line. We want to grow and change and experience wonderful new things in our lives. But the only way for growth on the top of the curve is for there to be discomfort on the bottom.

You see the dotted line on the bottom? We must dip down a little bit. We don't have to make giant strides all at one time. I didn't lift thirty-pound weights when I went back to the gym last year. I started with five-pound weights. The journey to lifting heavier weights was not without discomfort. It involved the repetition of lifting lighter weights over and over.

The growth on the top line is the outcome of the dip on the discomfort line. Growth is a natural result of doing something new and different, something challenging and beyond your comfort level. It will come at a cost. Allow yourself to be in a place where you are stretched, pulled, challenged, pushed. When I am challenging myself with a new weight or a new exercise, Tori, my coach, will say to me, "Christine, own it. Own that position."

Purposed Discomfort = Growth

You long to *own* a new level of growth. You joined me on this journey because you knew your soul needed a challenge. It longs to grow.

No one likes discomfort, but growth and discomfort are intricately connected.

I started out our adventure by inviting you to a life with paradox: The way forward is hard; the way forward is not hard. Living a life of bravery and joy. Now let's add a new layer to The Growth Wave. We are calling the discomfort line *Do the Work*. This is how you show up in new, brave ways in your life. The natural result of *Do the Work* is growth. We are calling the Growth line *Do the Joy*. When you drop below the line to do the work, then the joy comes. You receive the results of the work: new freedom, new connections, new growth.

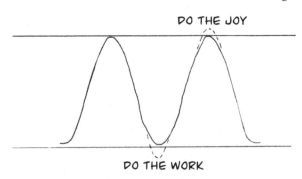

DO THE JOY

DO THE WORK

You are braver now than when we started. You have deeper access to joy than when we started. Soul adventurer, this is the growth wave at work.

− 13 −
SACRED BENEDICTION

A hard beginning maketh a good ending.

JOHN HEYWOOD

I was finishing my regular campsite evening routines: putting away extra gear in the bear box, boiling water to wash our faces, cleaning the coffee percolator to use in the morning. It was the final night of our thirty-three-day sabbatical trip around the United States.

Suddenly the unsolicited tears began.

God had designed a nighttime display of pure beauty on this final evening. It was a cool, quiet night. A brilliant round moon silhouetted the Rocky Mountains, the dark sky littered with stars. It was holy. Breathtaking. It felt like an incredibly divine gift created especially for us.

A sacred benediction.

The more I focused on the reality of these being the final routines of our final night, the heavier the tears fell. The more I grasped the perfect timing of this glorious nighttime display, the wetter my face became. I had many surprising tears along the way: when we crossed the California state line, when I saw Half Dome at sunset, when I witnessed the turquoise blue water in Crater Lake, Oregon. I felt God's lavish love for me in many small ways.

But on this night, the tears were spilling over from a bucket drawn from a deeper well. When Chris realized I was crying, he walked over. I collapsed into his arms, sobbing. We embraced under the dark sky. We stood there together, holding the month of memories, the experiences, the moment. Then we sat on the picnic table, looking up at the sky in complete silence, tears continuing to fall.

I was curious, attempting to name the source of my tears; however, it was a complex melting pot of emotion: gratitude, joy, awe, delight, wonder, fulfillment, love, contentment. Anxiousness about coming home. And some sadness. I didn't want it to be over, even though I knew we had a beautiful life to come home to.

I feel the same type of sacred benediction now as I'm typing.

The time has come for an end to our grand adventure together. I'm sitting outside at the farm table in my yard, watching the yellow leaves drift in the breeze. God orchestrated my favorite kind of day. It's perfect out here. The sky is vibrant blue, the air cool. There is a sacred quietness under the tall tree canopy.

I don't know how to say goodbye to you. This sacred benediction feels big. Heavy. Holy. I have faced one of the most challenging adventures of my entire life. It has been harder, more demanding, more shame-inducing than anything I have dared accomplish before. My words feel inadequate, like a microscopic drop of shallow words in an ocean of wisdom.

I needed this adventure. I needed to wander through the curvy roads of my soul. I needed to learn how to face my secrets, how to release myself into this great big world, with no expectations of what would happen next. Listening to my longing to write a book has forged me into being a better writer. Facing my fear of not being good enough developed in me the ability to admit my worth is settled. It is settled in something deeper, more eternal, more solid.

Last fall, Chris and I rented a campervan and camped through Maine and Nova Scotia. In Acadia National Park, the trails are marked with what they call blue blazes. The blue blazes are blue-painted marks on rocks and trees, about one inch wide, six inches long, guiding hikers along the path. We were on a sunrise hike up Cadillac Mountain, the highest point on the Atlantic coast and the first place to see the sun rise in North America. We hit the trail by 4:30 a.m. It was a perfectly clear morning, the gift of a glorious super moon illuminating the sky. The darkness made it a challenge to see where to go on the rocky trail. The only hope of making it to the top rested in two things: our headlamps and those blue marks. Our foreheads anxiously darted back and forth, up and down, desperately searching for the next blue mark.

We would stop, look for the clues, and continue. We searched with purpose. Every step. We did not want to miss the sunrise. Several times we missed the blue marks, veering way off course. Remember when I told you I tend to move fast? So does Chris. This means we are fast hikers, but also sometimes lost hikers.

Each time we turned back, we searched for the blue marks to get us back on the trail. Those marks led us where we needed to go.

I pray this book serves as a blue mark for you, showing you the path and guiding you on your journey. *I* want to live a life of bravery and joy. I know *you* want to live a life of bravery and joy. I am absolutely certain we can set the world ablaze with our unique adventures, each showing up in our lives in our distinctive ways. My hope is you will keep soul adventuring, even when you lose track of my blue marks. It's okay if my marks aren't helpful. This book has set me free from my need for you to need my marks. The freedom feels glorious, by the way. My hope is that this adventure has set you free to create your own way forward.

Other authors and teachers, leaders and counselors, coaches and pastors, are leaving blue marks for you too. Follow those if they are helpful. Your people are painting blue marks for you as well. Join them. Hey, create some blue mark adventures together and tag me. Better yet, invite me! Did you know I love going on adventures?

Listen closely now.

I mean this with as much seriousness as I can muster.

God is the ultimate Master Mark Maker, painting blue for you as often as you need it. He is the inventor of painting, the creator of blue, the author of all adventures. He is the mastermind behind mountains and the supplier of sunrises.

> ## We can set the world ablaze with our unique adventures.

Speaking of God, the time is right to clear something up. I wasn't the one who invited you on this journey. It was him all along. He invited you. I was nothing more than the envelope holding the invitation.

I almost quit and didn't do it. I'm grateful I kept at it. I believe more than ever that he wanted you to know of his heart for you and his desire for you to live a big, beautiful life.

As you consider how to find those blue marks, you only need to ask and look. He will show you the path ahead. He will also be with you on the path, which is the greatest promise of all.

Back to the story. We followed those blue marks with our headlamps to one of the most sacred experiences in all our travels. It awaited us as we rounded the corner out of the densely forested hike. I love what the Wabanaki people called the mountain: The White Rock of the First Light. The sun kissed the horizon, the pre-dawn light glowed on the water. We looked out across the expansive, sweeping view of the ocean. The large granite mountain created a natural amphitheater, as if God excitedly pats the ground and says to the world, "Hey, come sit down right here. I made a perfect little spot for you to watch my morning artistry." Even with our missteps and trail wanderings, we made it well before sunrise. When we sat down, a decent-sized crowd had already gathered.

Here is the sacred part.

It was perfectly, stunningly quiet.

Not a sound could be heard. Every person understood the sacredness of the moment, the need to revel in the beauty. I have never experienced anything like it. Silence and beauty, woven together to create a majestic display.

As I write these final words, I'm staring out at my yard, the same feeling of wonder filling my soul. It's quiet. My soul feels settled. The moment feels hallowed. My own little sacred benediction. Oh, the beauty of it all!

Soul adventuring with you has been one of the greatest treasures of my life. We both have brave and joy-filled lives to live. Now shut this book and get out there and find a new adventure! Maybe I'll see you somewhere along the path.

Christine

APPENDIX

BAG OF Tools for Calming Your Body

You may be wondering how to regain control once you have flipped your lid. The PFC is brought back online through calming practices. Think of the acronym **BAG OF**, like your own *bag of* tools, available to you anytime you need them. Your **BAG OF** tools are Breathe, Attention, Grounding, Outside, Friends.

B **reathe.** Deep, cleansing breath is an essential tool. Inhale four counts in through the nose, hold for four, and exhale through your mouth for four. Notice the gentle way the air feels coming in through the nose and then how calming the release feels as you blow it out of your mouth.

A **ttention.** Turn your attention away from the disturbing emotions and onto something peaceful to settle and calm your body. Look for beauty; it is a natural stress reliever for the body.

G **rounding.** Use the five senses to ground your body to this moment. Look for five colors, listen for four sounds, touch three items, smell two scents, taste one flavor. Tuning into your senses requires the brain to move out of the primitive functioning. Use the trick of *find your feet*. While breathing, notice your feet, feel them connected to your body and the ground.

Outside. Nature will calm the stress response system. If possible, touch something you see or put your bare feet directly on the ground or in the grass. Movement is an important part of calming exercises. If you are not able to move outside, find a window or turn on nature sounds on your phone or laptop.

Friends. Call or text someone to help calm you. Let them know you are struggling.

Expanding Your Window of Tolerance

When you are experiencing a distressing emotion, you can expand your Window of Tolerance by managing the dysregulation in your body. First, use the **BAG OF** tools from the Appendix. Those are always the go-to practices to begin calming yourself. Below are additional strategies for the two different branches of the autonomic nervous system.

For Hyperarousal (Sympathetic)

Since the brain's **accelerator** has been activated, your body needs slowing. Your body is stuck in the *up* energy (anxious, angry, high energy, fearful, panic, overwhelmed), and it needs to be brought down into your Window of Tolerance.

- Pay attention to the calming effect of the air as it enters your body.
- Gently tell yourself, "My body is on high alert, but I'm okay, and I can ride this wave. I'm learning how to care well for myself. I am feeling _____, and it's okay."
- Open your palms and notice the feelings of relaxation entering your body. Visualize yourself in a calming place where you are safe and secure.
- Find your feet and focus your attention on feeling the ground underneath you. If possible, take off your shoes and put your feet in grass.

For Hypoarousal (Parasympathetic)

Since the brain's **brake** system has been initiated, your body needs activation. Your body is stuck in the *down* energy (sluggish, numb, empty, withdrawn, blank), and it needs to be activated back up into your Window of Tolerance.

- Move your body. If you are sitting, stand up. March in place. Do big, long stretches, moving your arms over your head and to the right and left.
- Gently tell yourself, "My body is on high alert and disengaging to protect me. I'm safe, and it is okay to be connected to my body right now. I am feeling _____, and it's okay."
- Sometimes the slower breathing can make you feel more tired. Practice diaphragmatic breathing: Inhale deeply from your abdomen, then exhale forcefully.
- Splash cold water on your face, hold an ice cube, or drink ice water. Select an object within reach and describe what it feels like to hold it in your hand.

Story and Attachment

Here are questions to ask as you consider your story and attachment.

Attachment: Who lit up when I walked into the room? Who delighted in me? Who was happy to see me? How would I describe the types of attachments? How were conflicts resolved? Were they openly discussed or avoided? Were conflicts safe or scary? Reflect on the words safe, seen, soothed, and secure: Did this describe my experience?

Emotions: How did our family members communicate? Were they open or closed off? How were emotions expressed and handled? Were they openly discussed or suppressed? What stories are told about our family? How do these stories shape my understanding of our family's identity?

Recurring patterns and secrets: What are the recurring patterns of behavior, beliefs, and relationships? What types of addictions are there? Abuse? What were the roles and expectations of different family members? Were there any unspoken rules or hierarchies? Are there any family secrets that have been kept hidden? How might these secrets impact my understanding of my family?

Freedom Stories*

My Worth

- It is okay to be me.
- I am whole.
- I can be myself.
- I am resilient.
- I am significant.
- I matter.

My Relationships

- I am worthy of love.
- I am likeable.
- I belong.
- I am enough.
- I am lovable.
- I am important.
- I am supported.
- I can trust others.
- Others can see my weakness and still love me.

My Responsibility

- I can ask for help.
- I am okay the way I am.
- I deserve good in my life.
- It wasn't my responsibility.
- I am okay to be learning and growing.
- It wasn't my fault.
- It's okay to make mistakes.

My Safety

- I am brave.
- I am secure.
- I am safe.
- I am powerful.
- I am hopeful.
- It is okay to feel.
- I can stand up for myself.

* These Freedom Stories are adapted positive cognitions from the EMDR therapy protocol.

My Character

- I am capable.
- I am valuable.
- I can be trusted.
- I am intelligent.
- I can trust myself.
- I am honorable.
- I can ask for what I need.
- I am strong.

BIBLIOGRAPHY

Chapter 1

Thompson, Curt. *The Soul of Shame: Retelling the Stories We Believe About Ourselves*. InterVarsity Press, 2015.

Chapter 2

Wilder, Jim. "Joy Changes Everything." *Conversations Journal* 12.2 (2014): https://lifemodelworks.org/wp-content/uploads/2018/08/ Joy-Changes-Everything.pdf

Foster, Richard J. *Celebration of Discipline: The Path to Spiritual Growth*. HarperCollins, 1988.

Grant, Adam. "Being obsessed with happiness . . . ." X, August 28, 2024. https://x.com/AdamMGrant/status/1828841616460919069 ?mx=2.

Orwell, George. *Animal Farm*. 1st World Library, 2005.

Lewis, C. S. *Surprised by Joy*. HarperCollins Publishers, 2010.

Rene Descartes, philosopher, (1596–1650).

Smith, James K. A. *You Are What You Love: The Spiritual Power of Habit*. Baker Publishing Group, 2016.

Chapter 3

Nouwen, H. J. M. *The Wounded Healer: Ministry in Contemporary Society*. United Kingdom: PRH Christian Publishing, 2013.

Gilbert, Elizabeth. *Big Magic: Creative Living Beyond Fear*. Penguin Publishing Group, 2016.

Lewis, C. S. *The Lion, the Witch, and the Wardrobe*. Wyatt North Publishing, LLC, 2018.

Numeroff, Laura J. *If You Give a Mouse a Cookie*. HarperCollins, 2022.

Chapter 4

Maiberger, Barb. *EMDR Therapy Essentials: A Somatic Approach to Healing Trauma*. Integrated Body Mind Therapy, Inc. United States, 2019.

Socrates, (399 BC) philosopher.

Eagleman, David. *Incognito: The Secret Lives of the Brain*. Knopf Doubleday Publishing Group, 2011.

Forleo, Marie. *Everything Is Figureoutable*. Penguin Publishing Group, 2020.

Thompson, Curt. *The Soul of Shame: Retelling the Stories We Believe About Ourselves*. InterVarsity Press, 2015.

"Saints Among us: The Work of Mother Teresa." *Time*, December 29, 1975.

Cusick, Michael John, host. Restoring the Soul. Season 10, episode 229, "Dr. Todd Hall, 'The Connected Life,'" August 5, 2022. Podcast. https://restoringthesoul.com/restoring-the-soul-podcast.

Siegel, Dan. "Dr. Dan Siegel's Hand Model of the Brain." YouTube. August 9, 2017. https://youtu.be/f-m2YcdMdFw?si=RP -EcOn6PJpmEY2h.

Chapter 5

Young, Adam, host. The Places We Find Ourselves. "Why your family of origin impacts your life more than anything else" April 16, 2018. Podcast. https://youtu.be/Rn-HVk05Eu8?si=42 -wn4BCR9CmvscL.

Eagleman, David. *Incognito: The Secret Lives of the Brain*. Knopf Doubleday Publishing Group, 2011.

Chapter 6

Bericat, Eduardo. "The Sociology of Emotions: Four Decades of Progress," *Current Sociology* 64, no. 3, 2016.

Maté, Gabor. *In the Realm of Hungry Ghosts: Close Encounters with Addiction*. North Atlantic Books, 2010.

Rogers, Fred. *You Are Special: Neighborly Words of Wisdom from Mister Rogers.* Penguin Publishing Group, 1995.

Brown, Brené. *Rising Strong: How the Ability to Reset Transforms the Way We Live, Love, Parent, and Lead.* Random House Publishing Group, 2017.

Lerner, Harriet. *The Dance of Anger: A Woman's Guide to Changing the Patterns of Intimate Relationships.* HarperCollins, 2014.

Goleman, Daniel, Richard E. Boyatzis, Richard J. Davidson, Vanessa Druskat, and George Kohlrieser. *Achievement Orientation: A Primer.* United States: More Than Sound Productions, (n.d.).

Chapter 7

Cloud, Henry and John Townsend. *Boundaries: When to Say Yes, How to Say No, to Take Control of Your Life.* Zondervan, 2002.

Chapter 8

Rowling, J. K. *Harry Potter and the Chamber of Secrets.* Pottermore, 2015.

Brown, Brené. *Dare to Lead: Brave Work. Tough Conversations. Whole Hearts.* Random House Publishing Group, 2018.

Thompson, Curt. *The Soul of Shame: Retelling the Stories We Believe About Ourselves.* InterVarsity Press, 2015.

Glut, D. F. *The Empire Strikes Back: Star Wars: Episode V.* Random House Worlds, 1985.

Spurgeon, Charles. H. *Spurgeon's Sermons Volume 02: 1856.* Devoted Publishing, 2017.

Chapter 9

Willard, Dallas. *The Divine Conspiracy: Rediscovering Our Hidden Life In God.* HarperCollins, 2009.

Chapter 10

Maiberger, Barb. *EMDR Therapy Essentials: A Somatic Approach to Healing Trauma.* Integrated Body Mind Therapy, Inc. United States, 2019.

Lerner, Harriet. *The Dance of Anger: A Woman's Guide to Changing the Patterns of Intimate Relationships*. HarperCollins, 2014.

Thompson, Curt. *The Soul of Shame: Retelling the Stories We Believe About Ourselves*. InterVarsity Press, 2015.

Smith, James K. A. *You Are What You Love: The Spiritual Power of Habit*. Baker Publishing Group, 2016.

Wilder, Jim, Hendricks, Michel. *The Other Half of Church: Christian Community, Brain Science, and Overcoming Spiritual Stagnation*. Moody Publishers, 2020.

Chapter 11

Smith, James K. A. *You Are What You Love: The Spiritual Power of Habit*. Baker Publishing Group, 2016.

Palmer, Parker. J. *Let Your Life Speak: Listening for the Voice of Vocation*. United States: Wiley, 2024.

Neff, Kristin. *Self-Compassion: The Proven Power of Being Kind to Yourself*. HarperCollins, 2011.

Greenspan, Miriam. *Healing Through the Dark Emotions: The Wisdom of Grief, Fear, and Despair*. Shambhala, 2004.

Brown, Stuart. (2009) YouTube video, Ted Talks, "Play is More Than Fun".

Brown, Stuart and Christopher Vaughan. *Play: How it Shapes the Brain, Opens the Imagination, and Invigorates the Soul*. Avery, 2009.

Chapter 12

Lewis, C. S. *Mere Christianity*. United States: HarperCollins, 2009.

Palmer, Parker J. *Let Your Life Speak: Listening for the Voice of Vocation*. United States: Wiley, 2024.

Tournier, Paul. Translated by Edwin Hudson. *The Strong and the Weak*. Wipf & Stock Publishers, 2013.

MY SINCEREST
THANKS

Twenty-five years ago, I dreamt of writing a book titled *Mommy, I Dropped Your Bible in the Potty*. It was 1999, and my life was a daily dose of hilarity and exhaustion. We were raising three littles who were less than three years apart. Madison, four years old at the time, did drop my Bible in the toilet one lawless Sunday morning. I rescued the Bible but never penned the book. Ever since, Chris has been encouraging me to write a book. When my confidence faltered, Chris's belief in me only intensified. How blessed I am.

Chris, you are a good man, endlessly sacrificing for me to follow my unique God-given gifts. Our marriage is sturdy and beautiful. We have been etched by each other's annoying weaknesses and glorious strengths the way water erodes crevices in sturdy granite walls. It's a powerful process; deep change happening over long periods of time with slow, steady force. All I can say is a measly *thank you and I love you*. I am a better person because of your love for me. Even if we tried, we couldn't count the endless questions I asked about the outline, the number of subtitles we brainstormed, or the hours you drove while I wrote. There would be *no* book without you.

Mom and Dad, if I could possess even a fraction of your wisdom and grit, I would be one bold, smart woman. Our family tree is rich with both storytellers and learners, the combination forming deep structures in my soul. My family's penchant for tall tales shaped me into a woman who finds the punchline even before the whole story has unfolded. I'm equally grateful for the legacy of lifelong learning, imprinting on me the value of attempting new things.

Thanks to all my kids: Madison, Garrett, Landon, Colton, and Alyssa. From ping-pong to pickleball to late night chats, I love the way we are rich with love and abounding in laughter. I will never take for granted the joy of having adult kids who are my very dearest friends. The way you care about my life is a beautiful thing. Thank you for believing in me every step of the way. Nora and Ivey, thank you for making me the happiest Honey in all the world! May all of you grow in your love for Jesus and live brave and joy-filled lives.

A huge thank you goes out to my Lake House Posse: Heather Self, Jill Girling, Karla Harwell, Kristi Henderson, Shannon Upton, and Teri Farrell. You are the best friends a girl could ask for. I am incredibly grateful for the way each of you encouraged and championed me during this entire process. You were so confident I could do it. How could I be so blessed to have such a strong posse of capable, creative women like you on my side?

To my Wednesday Night Bible study: Thank you for being my guinea pigs, allowing me to hash out this material week after week. Your prayers and cheers kept me going. Thanks for listening to me complain about my writing misery and for allowing space for me to be human and work out my fears in real time with real people.

Thank you, Mona Parish, for all your insightful proofing, friendship, and constant cheerleading for this project. Your keen eye helped eliminate unnecessary words and ditch those bothersome parentheses.

Meredith, thank you for blazing the trail before me, showing fortitude by writing your beautiful book. Your consistent encouragement of, "I really, really get it" kept me going.

Thanks to the You Are Conference leadership team for trusting me to teach. Writing for *The Free One* and speaking at the 2021 conference was the beginning of my journey to confront my own ruts and roadblocks of shame. Through your invitations, God unearthed a reservoir of content I didn't even know existed.

I am truly humbled by the outpouring of support from many different friend groups: Bruce and Tamie, Chris and Ashley, neighbors Jake and Katy (who really know how to help a girl celebrate a rough draft completion), University Heights church family, Sarah and Steph (for your uncanny, timely texts along the way), Richard and Sarah (for the use of your lake house and your friendship and support), new CrossFit community, conference attendees, blog readers, and my brother Michael and niece Amanda. Your words of encouragement have touched my heart deeply, fueling my journey.

Thank you, Greg and Peter, for hosting me in your beautiful cottage in New Zealand for my week-long writing retreat. Writing while staring at your stunning view of the bay, on my second-story window writing perch, was the perfect backdrop to hash out the outline of this book. Let's be honest, our writing breaks at Omata Estate Winery were undoubtedly the best part of the process!

Thank you to Erin and the publishing team. I wavered in my belief in my ability to do it, and you kept cheering me on. Thanks for being an adventurer who wanted to see this adventure exist in the world.

To all my clients over the years, thank you for allowing me to be your sacred listener, holding space for your hurts, losses, wounds, and betrayals. I honor you. I do not take lightly the courage it takes to trust a stranger, much less a country girl from Arneckeville. Your bravery to seek healing and wholeness encourages me to do the same.

Finally, thank you to the consummate adventurer and creator Himself, the lover of my soul, Jesus. The way you left breadcrumbs along the rocky path for this weary traveler makes me solidly assured of your care for me. Thank you for showing me over and over how your love is better than life itself.

ABOUT THE AUTHOR

Christine Wolf Hoover, MA, LPC, is a passionate adventurer, living boldly and freely, driven by a desire to help others find that same freedom in Christ. As a trauma-informed therapist in private practice, she spends her days guiding people through the deep waters of their sacred stories. With more than twenty years of experience in Bible teaching, she articulates the vibrant life found in Christ with honesty and compassion, weaving biblical wisdom with her clinical expertise. Christine is deeply passionate about teaching at the intersection of emotional, relational, and spiritual health.

She has been married to Chris for more than thirty years. She adores their empty-nesting life and hanging with their three grown children and two granddaughters. She loves belly laughing, deep conversations, chips and salsa, time with friends and family, and planning her next adventures with Chris. Aging doesn't scare her—she knows each passing year only adds to her treasure trove of funny stories!

Connect with Christine at ChristineWolfHoover.com